Praise for *Missing Elem*

"*Missing Element Hidden Strength* me_
ist wisdoms with our modern quest for self-fulfillment. Filled with
spiritual and philosophical teachings presented in practical, accessible, and embodied ways, Tisha's book leads us into an investigation
of our own nature as a means of coming home to our wholeness."
—**Rachael Cohen, author of** *Everyday Plant Magic*

"A wonderful book filled with great quotes, insights, sidebars, graph-
ics, worksheets, and quizzes … I had such fun with this book—
learning, being reminded, and ultimately inspired. This is 'The Tao
of Creativity' in action, in book form where Tisha Morris shows you
the *Way*, with a capital W. She's offering up accessible, comprehen-
sive transformation at your fingertips. Read on and discover your
elemental self. Your hidden strengths are brewing deep within you,
just waiting to be shared. This book is your creativity catalyst inviting
you to apply these elemental insights to your life, in order for you to
become an even more beneficial presence on this earth!" —**Albert
Flynn DeSilver, author of** *Writing as a Path to Awakening*

"This book is a must have for spiritually minded entrepreneurs and
creatives/artists who want to energize or enhance their business or
creative process. I loved discovering my 'missing element,' and I'm
finding the simple ways the book suggests to power up my art and
business thrilling to implement! Get a copy and share it with your
creative community!" —**Sarah Bamford Seidelmann, author of**
How Good Are You Willing to Let It Get?

Missing
Element

• • • • •

Hidden
Strength

About the Author

Tisha Morris is an entertainment attorney and feng shui expert who has been featured on ABC's *Live with Kelly and Ryan*, *Hay House Radio* podcast, Today.com, *Elle Décor* magazine, ABC News, and *Well + Good* publication.

Tisha holds degrees in law, economics, and interior design and has certifications in feng shui, yoga, and business coaching. Tisha advises and represents clients using her entrepreneurial experience, legal and publishing expertise, intuition, and practical wisdom to help clients realize their potentials, clear blocks, and strategize for optimal success.

Tisha lives in Ojai, California, with her wife, poodle, and two step-cats. When not working with other creatives, she dreams of becoming a legal thriller novelist.

TISHA MORRIS

Missing Element

Hidden Strength

Apply the Natural Strength of All Five Elements to
Unlock Your Full Creative Potential

Llewellyn Publications
Woodbury, Minnesota

FIRST EDITION
First Printing, 2022

Book design by Christine Ha
Cover design by Kevin R. Brown
Interior art by the Llewellyn Art Department

Llewellyn Publications is a registered trademark of Llewellyn Worldwide Ltd.

Library of Congress Cataloging-in-Publication Data (Pending)
ISBN: 978-0-7387-7101-4

Llewellyn Publications
A Division of Llewellyn Worldwide Ltd.
2143 Wooddale Drive
Woodbury, MN 55125-2989
www.llewellyn.com

Printed in the United States of America

Also by Tisha Morris

Clutter Intervention
Decorating With the Five Elements of Feng Shui
Feng Shui Your Life
Mind, Body, Home

To Stella Ray,
my missing element and
hidden strength

Where you stumble,
there lies your treasure.

The very cave you are afraid to enter
turns out to be the source of
what you are looking for.

—*Reflections on the Art of Living:
A Joseph Campbell Companion*

Contents

Introduction

> If I have the belief that I *can* do it,
> I shall surely acquire the capacity to do it,
> even if I may not have it at the beginning.
> —Mahatma Gandhi

Within a few months, an invisible virus took down the world economy, business structures, our everyday routines, and hundreds of thousands of lives. Until a natural disaster occurs, it's easy to forget that we are only part of a bigger macrocosm that includes plants, oceans, animals, rocks, and microorganisms. Nature is always adjusting to find balance, and with either minor adjustments or cataclysmic disasters, she will achieve it. This pursuit of harmony and balance that nature relies upon is known as the Five Elements Cycle in Taoism.

The first time I was schooled on this idea of being part of something bigger was in sixth grade. Aside from playing the comic-relief troll in the school play, *The Hobbit*, I spent an entire semester creating an ecology notebook. None of us had heard of this subject, but all ninety-two of us preadolescents sat on the floor of the pod to watch filmstrips and lectures on the biodynamic intersection of humans, plants, and animals each day for an entire semester. By Christmas break, my reports, pamphlets, and notes

1

were neatly compiled in a red-clasped folder with the block letters ECOLOGY neatly stenciled on the front with help from my mom.

Looking back, I wonder if that immersive study of ecology was impactful in some way. Did it help precondition us to want to better the planet in some humanitarian sort of way? If so, it wasn't immediately apparent to me. As I left elementary school for junior high and beyond, I set my sights on how I could make a lot of money. I would become a lawyer. Meteorology didn't pay enough and being a stockbroker was too risky. Or maybe the other way around now.

I went to law school, made law review, clerked for two federal judges, and got a law job representing creditors in bankruptcy cases. It was at that point when I realized this wasn't what I wanted to do. Life screeched to a halt and took a left turn. Not only was I miserable in my job, but I was unhappy in my marriage too. This put into motion an entire renovation of my life, which led me to a 1920s home that also needed a renovation. It was through this process that I discovered my gift with working with the energy in homes and spaces. After obtaining a degree in interior design, I dove headfirst into all things spiritual, starting with yoga, then energy healing, and ultimately feng shui.

One of the foundational principles of feng shui is the Five Elements. As someone with an analytical mind, I loved any healing modality that explains energy in terms of categories. Around this time, I started seeing an acupuncturist who spoke the same language. That language being Chinese Medicine—the origin of acupuncture and feng shui. I began to see how my Five Elements balance (or lack thereof) in my body was mirrored in the Five Elements in my home. This led me to write the book *Decorating With the Five Elements of Feng Shui,* which shows how we can use

2

our home as a way to bring balance to our own energy using the Five Elements Cycle as our model.

What makes the Five Elements unique compared to other elemental systems is that it's the cycle of birth, death, and rebirth. More specifically, it's the creative process. It's the cycle that nature follows with its roots in Taoism. It's the cycle of being born, growing up, hitting midlife, slowing down, and ultimately dying. The Five Elements are also present in the microcosm as an energy system within our physical body. We are all made up of the same *five* elements through our organ systems, which is the foundation of acupuncture.

Maybe watching all those ecology filmstrips was impactful after all. It's difficult, if not impossible, to trace our winding paths through all the interconnected influences of coincidence, neural pathways, happenstance, astrology, and conscious choice. All these factors somehow led me from being an attorney to a feng shui expert.

What I do know is that our planet, in its current state of unrest, disharmony, and disregard for the interrelationship of humans and nature, can benefit from the ancient wisdom of Taoism, specifically the Five Elements Cycle, to create a win-win-win outcome: with ourselves, each other, and our planet. We are all being schooled on the fact that we are only a fraction of an entire ecosystem, not in control of it. We must work in harmony with each other and the planet, not in opposition. It starts with each of us, at home, in our relationships, and with our work in the world.

Whether it's our own creative project, a collaboration, or a team, the ecosystem of the Five Elements can enhance productivity, creativity, communication, and our overall satisfaction in life when used consciously. When we work in harmony with the

Tao by using the Five Elements, we create. We create something that's alive, and when in complete harmony, we create something that not only survives but thrives. That's when we go from childlike ego to childlike wonder. And we all get an A+ from the universe.

Your Missing Element Is the Key to Your Success

At certain points in our work or career, we reach a plateau. A plateau gives a momentary pause, a rest, from the climb. Any mountain climber appreciates a plateau, but then after the rest, it's time to keep going. It might be tempting to stay on the plateau, but eventually feelings of complacency, boredom, or unfulfillment creep in. The desire to stay comfortable is outweighed by the risk of moving beyond our comfort zone. This call to the next challenge is the beginning of what is commonly referred to as the hero's journey, a term coined by Joseph Campbell. It's common to refuse the call from the ordinary world into the unknown until pressures mount. The risk of not moving out of your comfort zone becomes more uncomfortable than that which was once comfortable. This well-known quote attributed to Anaïs Nin says it best: "And then the day came, when the risk to remain tight in a bud was more painful than the risk it took to blossom."

Refusing the call to go to the next level is always out of fear. Even if we're unaware of what we fear, our subconscious knows. Once we can name it, it's then that we can do something about it. When you face the fear, you transform it and concurrently unlock a hidden treasure within that allows you to reach new heights. This is what Joseph Campbell referred to when he said, "The very cave you are afraid to enter turns out to be the source of what you are looking for."[1]

If you feel like you've reached a plateau in your work or in any area of your life, the good news is that you haven't reached what you're capable of doing and achieving. By embracing these unknown territories within, you start to integrate new aspects of yourself that you were, up to now, either consciously avoiding or unconsciously unaware. These aspects are your inner Water, Wood, Fire, Earth, and Metal elements.

We all have at least one of the elements that comes naturally to us and one that is our Achilles' heel, which we'll refer to as your *missing element*. For example, people with a missing Metal element skip over the details necessary in the Metal phase and end up with unfinished projects. Or maybe it's the fear of being seen that's integral to the Fire phase. For those with a missing Wood element, seeing the big picture may be challenging, and thus, you're left without a plan to take that first step. Others skip over the time needed for integration that the Earth element provides, which results in not receiving the monetary compensation desired. And in our busy world, it's challenging for those lacking the Water element, or any of us, to not take the time and space needed for inner reflection that the Water element requires.

At this point, you may be thinking, *Shouldn't I focus on my strengths?* Absolutely. We have access to all five elements, but there's one element we lead with or that comes most naturally to us. That's your *primary element*. Consider it your bread and butter or the softball life throws you. My former acting teacher would say, "You get that for free," when it was a character trait we already embody that our character also had. In other words, we didn't have to put in extra work for that quality to come through the role. Instead, we needed to focus on the traits that weren't native to ourselves.

While it's important to know your strengths, this book focuses on accessing and integrating aspects of ourselves that don't come so easy. By integrating all aspects of ourselves, we create on a bigger level than ever before, not to mention experience more satisfaction and fulfillment in our life. We're going for self-mastery and successful collaborations. In doing so, we play to our strengths, but we also embrace our weaknesses. I call this *upleveling*.

Your missing element has been the missing piece that's kept you at a certain plateau of success. Your missing element has likely tripped you up time after time and kept you from reaching the level of success of which you're capable. Until now, you might have thought you didn't have what it takes to achieve a certain goal, or the timing was off, or something you wanted must not be "meant to be." Now, you'll be able to name your missing element and learn to work with it, and then all those old stories will be in the past. It's time to reclaim it, transform it, and elevate your game to the next level. As we embrace our missing element, we not only become more whole, but we also become more fulfilled.

The more whole we are within ourselves, the less we seek and need from others. That, of course, doesn't mean we all become lone wolves. I'm suggesting the contrary. When we put our happiness, our fulfillment, our reliance, in the hands of others, it sets us up for disappointment, unrealized expectations, and even failure. Instead, the goal should be interdependence. When we rely on others to complete us in personal or professional relationships, we're relying on a dependence that can be taken away at any time. On the other hand, interdependence is expansive with infinite potential for everyone involved. This book will help you fill in your missing element, not only to uplevel your own work, but to also contribute more effectively to collaborations.

All of us are engaged with all Five Elements each day simply through our daily routine, but some elements we embrace more than others. For example, I love starting new things and tend to have several balls in the air at once, whereas someone else may prefer working on a single-focus project for the day. Some people thrive on taking something that already exists and making it better. Or maybe you're someone who prefers taking a supportive role by helping others accomplish their goals. If that's you, thank you, Earth element.

For business owners, your missing element may be those moving parts you hire out. We're not meant to be an expert in all things, which is why we have diverse occupations and work as an ecosystem. If you think about it, it's quite extraordinary how we each have gifts and talents that intertwine with one another. We each get to do what we love and can collaborate with others to do what they love.

But what happens when you can't hire out, either for monetary constraints or feasibility? Or when it's a solo project that you want complete autonomy over? I recently helped a woman publish her book, and she didn't want any outside editing because she channeled it from her guides. I think all creative media are forms of channeling and too many cooks in the kitchen can dilute the essence of our work at times. When a painting, a dance, a book, or a business is our unique manifested creation, what an extraordinary experience and resulting product it can be. Think of some of our greatest artists and inventors and their solo creations, such as Leonardo da Vinci, Thomas Edison, Nikola Tesla, William Shakespeare, Georgia O'Keeffe, and Jane Austen.

We all have the ability to create a masterpiece from idea to completion. Will it be easy? Of course not. Will you want to quit halfway through? Maybe. Will you question yourself along the way? Most likely. Will you rub up against uncomfortable places within yourself? Yep. Will it be worth it? Absolutely.

How You Will Cultivate Your Hidden Strength

In this book, you will get to know your primary element—where your strengths lie. You'll also get to know your missing element—where your potential goldmine is held. You'll discover easy ways to awaken this aspect within yourself and become familiar with it by incorporating the missing element into your workspace, daily activities, and even your wardrobe. Yes, you'll be feng shui-ing your office, your closet, and your life to become the complete package. As a result, your relationships will improve, the quality of your work will be enhanced, and you will finally reach the goals you've set but weren't able to meet for reasons unknown until now.

In part 1, you will learn how the Five Elements Cycle and the creative process are one and the same. The creative process is how we go from idea to completion, or intangible to tangible, of anything physical that we use and enjoy here on Earth. Similar to how we are born from spirit into matter, so too is the process of an idea into a physical form. Chapter 2 breaks the elements down to give you the energetic qualities of each, while chapter 3 takes you through the creative cycle that is an integral part of your everyday life. The creative process is broken down into its five phases that can be applied to any project or vocation, from yoga to writing.

In part 2 we transition from the Five Elements as a cycle we find in our everyday life to using the Five Elements as a personality system. You will learn the characteristics of each of the elements as they present themselves in how we run our energy and how they show up in our personalities. You'll be able to recognize and activate more fully these energies that already reside within you. To give you a preview, the Water element is your inner guru; the Wood element is your inner leader; the Fire element is your inner motivator; the Earth element is your inner stabilizer; and the Metal element is your inner organizer. Meet your board of directors available to you at any time.

In chapter 4, you'll discover your primary element by taking the Five Elements Quiz. This quiz will show you how you rank among all five elements, from strongest to weakest. You could probably make a list right now of your strengths and weaknesses, but you've most likely never done this in context of the Five Elements, or as it pertains to the creative cycle. You will quickly see where you've run into challenges in the creative process in the past and how to now overcome them.

You've also likely never taken advantage of all Five Elements, to which you have complete access. Chapter 5 introduces you to your inner board of directors available to you at any time. Once you understand the role each element plays in your life, you'll be prepared to use all Five Elements when needed. Chapter 6 focuses on the element or elements in which you scored the lowest so that you can begin to integrate it into your daily life. It's here where you can make the biggest changes and leaps in your life. Chapters 7 through 11 provide practical ways to cultivate each of the elements in order to turn your missing element into your hidden strength.

While part 2 shows you how to integrate all the elements within yourself, part 3 expands the Five Elements beyond yourself to show how to use them to enhance the creative process in collaborations and teams. It's here where you learn to create dynamic duos and powerful collaborations using the Five Elements as your guide. When a partnership is the right fit, it has the potential to exceed what one person can do on one's own. Think Charles and Ray Eames, Elton John and Bernie Taupin, and the Wright brothers. They don't complete one another; they bring out the gold in each other to create a third creation. In chapter 12, see how each element partners with the other elements and how they create together.

In chapter 13, it's time to create your dream team. Every manager should follow what basketball coaches strategically know in creating their team of five players. It's Team Five Elements. If you manage a team of people, you'll want to have all the elements represented for more harmony, increased productivity, and a greater level of success.

Chapter 14 shows you how to apply the Five Elements as a workplace system that fits your business. Whether you're an artist, a solo entrepreneur, or a corporate team leader, you'll learn practical ways to integrate the Five Elements Method as a system for efficiency, flow, creativity, camaraderie, invention, cooperation, and success that exceeds what has currently been achieved in the workplace based on outdated structures.

We've been handed a unique time in history when we get to redefine how we create for ourselves and with others, at home and in the workplace. It's time to integrate the ancient wisdom handed down thousands of years ago based on nature's cycles of flow, ease, harmony, cooperation, and support to uplevel businesses and the resulting products and services.

Which element has kept you from living your life to the fullest or reaching the level of success of which you're capable? Which element are you ready to embrace more fully? Thus far, you've gotten by with only utilizing two or three of the elements. We're at an inflection point on the planet where we must go beyond what we've been capable of creating in the past. Are you ready to create something amazing and life changing, not to mention soul fulfilling? Your missing element holds the key to a deeper sense of purpose and a greater level of impact you can have in the world. It's time to turn your missing element into your hidden strength.

PART 1

Integrating the Five Elements in Your Everyday Life

CHAPTER 1

Applying Taoist Principles to Our Modern Life

> In dwelling, live close to the ground.
> And thinking, keep it to the simple.
> And conflict be fair and generous.
> And governing, don't try to control.
> And work, do what you enjoy.
> And family life, be completely present.
> —*Tao Te Ching*, translated by Arthur Waley

Taoism is an ancient Eastern philosophy with origins dating back over five thousand years ago, as shamans living along the Yellow River in northern China explored ways of living in accordance with the primordial energy that connects us with spirit and earth, known as the *Tao*. Taoism is a philosophy used "to enhance the re-integration of individual beings with their total environment of time and space and energy."[2] In other words, Taoism breaks through a false sense of duality for the purpose of reuniting oneself with universal physical and spiritual energies.

According to Taoist principles, human beings are a microcosm of the universe. You may be familiar with the metaphor that we are each a drop of water from the same ocean. If so, then you've already been introduced to ancient Taoism. To take this concept further, Taoists see themselves as part of the patterns of rhythm of all that exists.³ This is the *Tao*, or the "Way," meaning the more you are in sync with the macrocosmic patterns of energy, the more you will experience flow and harmony in your own life. Another common adage that sums up this principle is "go with the flow."

Taoism was also perhaps the original precursor of mind-body holistic principles as it made no separation of the mind, body, and spirit. In fact, it was the origin of what later became known as Chinese Medicine. It is through Chinese Medicine that the pillars of Taoism have made their way to the West through modalities such as acupuncture, feng shui, and qigong. It was my studies in feng shui that led me to understand and appreciate Taoist philosophies and how to incorporate them into our home and in our everyday life.

In addition to cultivating health and longevity, Taoist philosophies were also used as a template for leadership within communities. To achieve harmony, all persons "with naturally good and high energy" contributed to their community without any rivalry, while emperors used "their virtues" for good and without the need for force.⁴ Taoism began to take on a more formal teaching when the treatise known as the *Tao Te Ching* was introduced by the sage Lao Tzu. The *Tao Te Ching* is a highly revered text in Taoism that translates to "The Way of Integrity" and is said to have been authored by Lao Tzu, along with translations by Confucius, over two thousand years ago. Its eighty-one verses continue to be translated and read today because of the universality of its wisdom regarding right action.

The *Tao Te Ching* described methods of cultivating Taoism as a lifestyle into physical and mental techniques, such as meditation, martial arts, and alchemy. Like most philosophies and practices based in truth, politics and power took over the use of Taoism around the first century. However, a new use of Taoism emerged in the form of a divination tool. With the concept of *change* being at the root of Taoism, scholars began using Taoism as a tool of seeing and appreciating the patterns of change through the mystical book, known as the *I Ching*.

The Evolving *I Ching*

The primary text that codifies the concepts of Taoism is the *I Ching*, which translates to "The Book of Changes," and is considered to be the oldest book ever written. However, it probably doesn't read the way you think. In its original form, it's simply lines. Perhaps it's the original binary code, except instead of two lines, it's three lines called trigrams. Thousands of years later, the three lines were expanded into six lines, called hexagrams. These hexagrams are the basis of what we now know as the *I Ching*.

The *I Ching* was the first text to introduce the concept of yin and yang. Because of the universality of their meanings, the words *yin* and *yang* have been integrated into our Western language. The phrase "You are the yin to my yang" is a common adage in terms of relationships. Marked by the common yin-yang symbol, the two polarities intertwine to create one circle. The concept of yin and yang can be found in every area of life on planet earth: heaven and earth, day and night, hot and cold, active and passive, left and right, front and back, Republican and Democrat, Apple and Android, Lyft and Uber, and the list goes on. Another common way to think of this duality is in terms of masculine and feminine energies.

Masculine and feminine energies are distinguishable from male and female or man and woman, as we all have aspects of masculine and feminine energies within us. In fact, our left brain, which controls the right side of our body, is considered the masculine side while the right brain, which controls our left side, is the feminine side. Masculine energy is yang and responsible for our analytical and logical mind, while the feminine energy is yin and allows for creativity and intuition.

The *I Ching* further explores the relationship of energy and introduces us to the Five Elements. If yin and yang were the parents of energy, the Five Elements would be their children. Each hexagram is associated with a quality of energy ranging from the most yin (six broken lines) to the most yang (six solid lines) and every range of energy between these two polarities. The original eight trigrams are the foundation of the commonly used tool in feng shui known as the Bagua Map. The Bagua Map (also referred to as the Pa Kua) is a specific arrangement of these original eight trigrams, and when overlayed over a space, usually a floor plan, it reveals the energetic qualities of those spaces. Five of the eight original trigrams are represented by the Five Elements. Although the *I Ching* has endured hundreds of translations since its inception thousands of years ago, the shortened translation of the Five Elements as trigrams is generally accepted as the following:

Wood: The Arousing

Fire: The Clinging

Earth: Standstill

Metal: The Joyous

Water: The Abysmal

The translation of each trigram gives us the essence of the elements in their purest form and will be explored in more detail in the next chapter.

The Wisdom of the Five Elements

The energetic essence of each of the Five Elements has been interpreted by Chinese scholars, with the most widely accepted translation being passed down from the Chinese emperor Confucius. It is said that Confucius stood by the river and said, "Isn't life's passing just like this, never ceasing day or night," referring to the idea of change, which is the basis of the *I Ching* and the Five Elements.[5]

All sixty-four of the hexagrams create the spectrum of energies ranging from the most yin to the most yang. Of those sixty-four energies, the five trigrams that represent the Five Elements make up the cycle of birth, death, and the three stages in between. In other words, it's the cycle of creation. The creative process of turning thoughts into things is the Five Elements Cycle. Each element is essential to the creative process and responsible for conception, growth, achievement, maintenance, and letting go. This cycle allows for the continuance of life on our planet at a sustainable rate.

To understand the Five Elements Cycle, it's best to look to nature as our teacher. Nature doesn't have to think about the Five Elements because it is the Five Elements Cycle. Nature births, grows, dies, and regenerates in accordance with the Five Elements Cycle, which can be cataclysmic at times. It doesn't take sides and certainly doesn't accommodate to our human comforts.

Do humans affect the Five Elements balance on the planet or are we at the mercy of nature's Five Elements balance? This question is the core issue of climate change discussions. I believe the answer is both. People, plants, rocks, animals, lava—and, yes, even viruses—must all coexist and cohabitate. The more we work in tandem with one another, the more harmonious our existence will be. This is the basis of Taoism—to be in flow with nature because we are part of nature. To be anything else is a form of resistance, the opposite of the Tao.

In the following chapter, we'll explore the characteristics of each of the Five Elements to see how each element plays a necessary role in the cycle of birth, death, and rebirth. With each element being unique with its own characteristics, all five are essential for the completion of the creative cycle. You will begin to see how these ancient principles, so basic at their core, are essential to our continued existence on planet Earth, as well as a parallel to our own process of creativity and cocreation.

CHAPTER 2

Discovering the Five Elements

Heaven is high, the earth is low; thus the
Creative and the Receptive are determined.

—*I Ching*

According to Taoism, the Five Elements are the building blocks for all energy and physical manifestations created therefrom. Other Eastern and Western philosophies and sciences have also used elements as a foundational principle; for example, the four elements in astrology, the three elements in Ayurveda, and the seven elements associated with the chakras in yoga. While there is some overlap in terminology and similarities in energetic qualities, what differentiates the Five Elements from other element systems is that the Five Elements work together to create a cycle or a circle.

The Circle of Life

A circle has no beginning or ending and is often used as a symbol for unity, wholeness, and eternity. The Five Elements Cycle is in essence a circle that embodies the creative cycle starting with birth and ending with death. In other words, it's the process that all matter goes through, including the impermanence of our time on Earth in a human body. Another way to think of a circle is as a spiral. The spiral, particularly when presented in the Fibonacci sequence, is considered to be the seed point and continuing evolution of life. The Five Elements Cycle can be seen as a spiral as we continue to pass over the cycles at a sustainable growth rate.

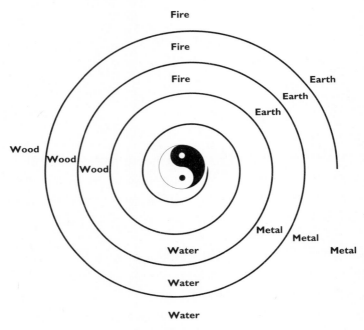

Figure 1. The Five Elements Cycle of Life

While each element has characteristics common to other elemental systems, it's how each element works in relation to each other that is the differentiating factor. In the same way all five players on a basketball team have their specific talent and role, they must also work together. Similarly, each element has its specific job and also needs the others for creation and expansion to take place. Each plays its unique role for the greater good of the whole team. The Five Elements Cycle is the perfect template for organizations with each team player contributing their best for the good of the whole.

Each of the Five Elements can be analyzed individually, which we will do throughout the book, but it is the wisdom of the Five Elements Cycle that makes this elemental system extraordinary. It is the cycle of creation with each element being an integral phase of the cycle. When you create something "out of thin air" or create things from thoughts, you are describing the Five Elements Cycle. When you create something that becomes uber-successful, then you've created it using all Five Elements harmoniously without even realizing it. Whereas if you've created something that barely got off the ground, if at all, then you stumbled upon an unexecuted phase of the Five Elements Cycle. By the end of this book, you'll know exactly which element you glossed over and how you can incorporate it in future projects for success.

As we make our way through the characteristics of each element, you can think of each element literally, metaphorically, or symbolically. All are true. For example, the Wood element includes what you would think of as wood, such as a tree, but it's also represented energetically in a variety of ways, including as a season, a color, an organ system, and even a shape. In chapter 4, we'll also expand our analysis to include our human personalities. Within any of these characteristics, however, you'll notice common themes, whether they're presented in terms of gardening, writing a book, or what you're wearing. Simply put, everything on our planet is made up of the Five Elements, literally and symbolically. Once you understand their basic characteristics, you will see the world in terms of the Five Elements or a combination of them. Let's take a closer look at the characteristics of each element.

The Water Element

Water is considered the birthplace of creation for living beings, from microorganisms to the watery placenta of a mother's womb. Humans consist of at least 60 percent water with our brain being 70 percent, our lungs 80 percent, and our blood 80 percent. Similarly, Planet Earth is made up of 70 percent ocean water, making it a habitable and fertile planet for life. In the Five Elements Cycle, the Water element represents the conception of something new. It is the phase from which all is birthed. The circle of life depicted by the Five Elements also comes to a completion in the Water phase. Thus, the Water element is the beginning and end of creation. All projects and ideas begin in the Water phase and come to completion in the Water phase.

Each element is traditionally represented by a season in Taoism. Just as the circle follows the cycle of birth, death, and rebirth, so does our annual calendar as it passes through the seasons each year. The Water element is associated with winter, when most living things die or go dormant. However, it's also the season of rebirth when new seeds are planted. You will not see the seeds as they are under the soil. Any visible manifestation of those seeds will be a few months away in the Wood element phase.

Similar to planting a seed, think about when an idea comes. We usually sit and think on it before taking action. This could be for a few minutes, a couple of hours, or many months, if not years, depending on how big the idea. This time of inactivity before the seed begins to sprout in the Wood phase is the Water phase. The winter, or Water element phase, is the metaphorical dark of night just before the sun rises, when the veil between heaven and earth is the thinnest. It's here where we receive insights, ideas, and information. The information you download in the shower or the *aha* that comes out of nowhere represents the Water element. In our busy world, we generally avoid this phase and opt instead for the external world of distractions. However, there is so much power to access in the Water phase, and it is often the secret behind the success of visionaries, inventors, and changemakers.

As winter moves into spring, we start to see physical manifestation of the seeds planted. Animals come out of hibernation. Flower buds make themselves seen and green grass starts to root from seemingly nowhere. There is movement. Despite our temperature-controlled lifestyle, we too come out of hibernation. It tends to be a time of year when we take action on ideas and introspections that we ruminated over during the dark of winter. And with that first action step begins the rest of the Five Elements cycle, not too unlike that of a hero answering the call to her next journey.

Characteristics of the Water Element in Taoism

Season: Winter

Time of Day: Midnight

Color: Black

Climate: Cold

Direction: North

Stage of Development: Birth and Death

Organ Network: Kidney

The Wood Element

The moment you took your first breath was your first experience with the Wood element. Like the flower peeking through the safety of its bud on the first day of spring, so too did you upon leaving your mother's womb, seeing the light of the world while being lifted from the belly. We all signed up for a hero's journey by being born and taking off into this unknown world. The energy created and stored in the Water phase transforms into physical form in the Wood phase, and, thus, it's the first element that reveals itself in physical, visible form. The Wood element takes the idea that was gestated in the Water phase and converts into our physical reality. This is the essence of the spiritual becoming physical. The Wood phase is an essential element or step for the beginning of anything new, whether it is a business plan, a story outline, or drawing the blueprints for a house. It starts with simply putting an idea onto paper.

In physical form, the Wood element shows up in nature as actual wood in the form of a tree or plant. Like all the elements, it can also present itself symbolically as a color and shape. The Wood element is represented by the color green and its shape is columnar or linear to mimic the upward-growing energy of a tree. Whether in its literal or symbolic form, the Wood element is the energy of growth and expansion. Of course, a tree must sustain certain environmental conditions to grow. This is where we can start to see the interrelationship of the Five Elements. A tree or plant must be properly rooted. In other words, it needs the literal grounding of dirt (Earth element). A tree also needs water (Water element) and sun (Fire element), and the dirt must have the proper nutrients (Metal element) to support its successful growth.

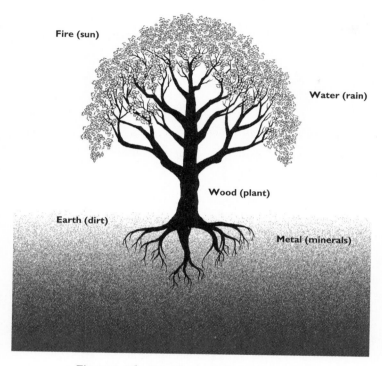

Figure 2. The Five Elements Cycle in Nature

When a tree has all these components, it not only survives, but thrives. It can also sustain strong winds or other weather challenges. The same is true for us as we weather the storms in our life. The tree must be strong, yet flexible, not too unlike a baby's skull as it crosses the threshold of the womb into its new world. The Wood element is adaptable in order to navigate these new situations life throws our way. Like priming the pump, the Wood energy starts to move and gains momentum as it enters the Fire phase, where the full manifestation of energy is then realized.

Characteristics of the Wood Element in Taoism

    Season: Spring

    Time of Day: Sunrise to mid-morning

    Color: Green

    Climate: Wind

    Direction: East

    Stage of Development: Childhood

    Organ Network: Liver

The Fire Element

When I was a kid, there was nothing more exciting than the last day of school. I felt so free as I jumped off the steps of the school bus and ran home as fast as I could. Nothing but sunshine ahead. This is when the Wood phase moves into the Fire phase. As spring turns to summer, the heat intensifies and then reaches its highest expression of energy at the height of summer. To my thirteen-year-old self, this is when my sunburn finally turned into a tan.

The Fire element is the phase of a project in which we pour most of our energy. In terms of writing a book, it's cranking out the 80,000 words of your manuscript. For a film, it's the two weeks of shooting around the clock to get all the necessary footage. It's pure exertion of life force energy that moves through us. That is, until we burn out. For those who have their primary element in Fire, this is the phase in which they thrive and tend to *go go go* until they crash.

The Fire element is the element that our caffeinated, consumer driven culture tends to gravitate to the most. Having more energy is something that many of us strive for to accomplish everything we need to get done in a given day. Think of the sunny, warm day when you have tons of energy. If only this level of energy was sustainable. For most of us, excluding essential workers, our inner Fire element was sidelined in 2020 when we were forced to stay home. Many turned to nature and exercising inside and outside to exert some Fire energy.

The Fire element also represents the time of life when we look and feel our best. While this is arbitrary depending on a number of factors, the Fire element phase in general is usually just before we hit mid-life. From there, our energy levels start to decrease and for women it can be the beginning of menopause when hormones change and energy begins to deplete. On the macro level, this marks the end of the overall Fire phase of life. That being said, we contain the Fire element within us at all times as it is our life force energy.

As the heat comes to a peak in late summer, it plateaus. It reaches its height given the conditions of the sun and its accessibility to Earth. As I write this, a volcano is erupting in Iceland. Thousands of years of fire underground finally reached its zenith and must break through and release its built-up magma. When the lava cools, it creates new land. This is an example of the Five Elements cycle in its literal form in nature. We must release our energy, gradually or perhaps spewing it out after a long buildup, for regeneration of something new to begin. When we don't flow with these cycles, we end up spinning our wheels, and eventually it takes a toll on our health. The only question is at which elemental phase are we blocking our own flow.

The Fire element phase gives way to the Earth element. This is when we start thinking about the end of summer and kids somewhat reluctantly start looking forward to going back to school again. But there's still a few more weeks of summer vacation left to relax. Welcome to the stabilizing Earth element.

Characteristics of the Fire Element in Taoism

    Season: Summer

    Time of Day: Noon

    Color: Red

    Climate: Heat

    Direction: South

    Stage of Development: Adolescence to early adulthood

    Organ Network: Heart

The Earth Element

For regions with seasonal climates, there's a gap between summer ending and fall not yet arriving. It's here where we enter the Earth phase. In the Northern Hemisphere, it's the months of August and September. It's that time of year when events also stagnate. Professional sports are in between seasons. As a kid, I remember August was a tough month. Spending days at the pool and playing tennis had become rote, first-world problems. But I wasn't quite ready to go back to the structured school day either, which you can probably guess is the Metal element phase.

The Earth element is the transition from active energy, *yang* energy, to passive energy, *yin* energy. While the Wood and Fire elements exert energy and the Water and Metal elements diminish energy, the Earth element grounds energy. The Earth element is associated with late summer or early fall; however, it's technically considered to be the fall and spring equinoxes when light (yang) and dark (yin) are exactly equal. It is a moment of equilibrium on our planet of masculine and feminine energies. In the *I Ching*, it's referred to as a *stillpoint*—where there is no movement of energy.

When there's no movement, as is the case with the Earth phase, life can feel a bit boring. For this reason, it's easy to overlook the benefits of the Earth element despite it being an essential phase of the creative process. When you take a moment to relax into the Earth element, you can feel a sense of peace, grounding, and harmony. So is the case when we reach the Earth phase in midlife. As we slow down, we begin to relax into life and experience it with more inner peace and tranquility.

The Earth element occurs in its natural form as dirt or clay. In its symbolic form, it is represented in earth tones, such as brown, orange, and yellow. Its shape is square or rectangular, which holds the grounded energy of the four corners. You can think of a square table, the four corners of a house, or the rectangle container garden in which you plant herbs or vegetables.

In using a tree as an example of the Five Elements Cycle, the Earth element holds the tree in place and gives it a space from which to grow. While the Earth element prefers the status quo, it allows the other elements to do their work. In other words, the Earth element is the stage on which all the other elements get to play. You can most likely identify an Earth element person in your life, if not yourself, who is the grounded, nurturing type who doesn't take a lot of credit and yet is indispensable for the space they hold for others to shine.

The peace-loving Earth phase may seem idyllic and perhaps it is; however, energy must continue to move in order for evolutionary changes to occur, also known as life on Earth. From the Earth phase, energy begins to decrease as it moves into the Metal phase. It may seem paradoxical, but contraction of energy is essential for expansion to occur. This is the underestimated role of the Metal element.

Characteristics of the Earth Element in Taoism

Season: Late summer; fall and spring equinoxes

Time of Day: Afternoon

Color: Yellow / orange

Climate: Humidity

Direction: Center

Stage of Development: Middle age

Organ Network: Spleen

The Metal Element

As we move into autumn, the supple, green leaves turn into crisp colors as the days get shorter. As the planet tilts away from the sun, there's a ripple effect of the diminishing energy that affects nature and its inhabitants. In terms of the twenty-four-hour day, Metal is represented as dusk when there's just a glimmer of sunlight left before darkness falls. In our life cycle, this is our silver years when we've still got just enough energy to stay active. It's interesting that the word *silver* is often used in association with the retirement years and is also the literal form of the Metal element.

The Metal phase is a yin phase in which energy is withdrawn, but it's important to note that while energy dissipates in the Metal phase, it's not random. Instead, it's a process of refinement. The Metal element is the ultimate organizer and purifier of energy. It separates the wheat from the chaff. It refines, organizes, and purifies energy so that only the best is left to be used. It reveals the diamond in the rough or the gold standard. It's no wonder that precious metals have historically been a store of value for money, perhaps only to be replaced by technology that is reliant on precious metals.

The Metal element in its literal form consists of rocks and all metals, including precious metals and gemstones. The Metal element is symbolically represented by white, gray, and metallic colors, along with circular or oval-shaped objects. It's no coincidence that precious metals are used for their intricate and detailed properties in high-level electronics and technologies where precision is essential.

Those who have their primary element in Metal have a refined taste in aesthetics with quality reigning over quantity. The Metal phase is an obvious, necessary step for those dominant in the Metal element, but it's often a necessary evil for other element types. Without the Metal element we would have an abundant of superfluous information produced in the Fire phase with potentially no organization. The Metal phase is the editing-out phase to determine what belongs and where it goes. Cue Marie Kondo.

As the days become shorter and the nights grow colder, fall turns to winter and the Metal phase ends where we began— in the Water phase. While birth begins in the Water phase, something must first die for regeneration to occur. The Five Elements is complete only to begin again with each round of the spiral being a form of expansion.

Do you ever feel like you come around to the same issues in your life that you thought were resolved? We are always growing along our soul's spiral of expansion through the phases at our own pace. With each pass around the spiral, we have a renewed awareness with more expansion as a result. When we neither rush nor stagnate through life, we meander along our path. To *meander* is the intersection of yin and yang energy and the ultimate goal in feng shui. It's there that we find our flow through the Five Elements Cycle and find ourselves living with the Tao.

Characteristics of the Metal Element in Taoism

Season: Autumn

Time of Day: Dusk

Color: White, silver

Climate: Dryness

Direction: West

Stage of Development: Senior

Organ Network: Lung

CHAPTER 3

Using the Five Elements to Master the Creative Process

> A successful creative career is always built on successful creative failures. The trick is to survive them.
> —Julia Cameron, *The Artist's Way*

Now that you're familiar with the characteristics and role of each element, let's take a closer look at how the elements work together to form a template for the creative process. Nature is our master teacher to whom we can always look in understanding the Five Elements Cycle of creative energy. Before there were clocks or calendars, humans had a sense of time by watching the sun rise and set each day, the monthly moon cycle, and the planets and constellations systematically putting on a show. This passage of time via nature—daily, monthly, annually, and our own life cycle—is in essence the Five Elements Cycle. It's also the cycle we use in every area of our life, from daily activities, such as exercising and cooking, to major events in our life, including starting a relationship or creating a business.

In the following sections, you'll see how the Five Elements Cycle is the structure underlying all processes. The examples I've provided are only a sampling, but the same analysis can be applied across the board to any area of life. We'll start with a cycle we're all familiar with but perhaps haven't thought of in terms of the Five Elements Cycle, and that's the moon phases.

Five Elements in the Moon Phases

In 2021, a cargo ship was stuck in the Suez Canal for six days, creating global supply issues for consumer goods. Officials had to look up to the sky for answers. They waited for the full moon in order for the tide to rise enough to give the ship extra buoyancy to become unstuck. The moon phases affect rivers, oceans, our bodies, our emotional cycles, and yes, even cargo shipping. The moon phases are also synonymous with the Five Elements phases.

The moon cycle starts with the new moon, when the moon passes between Earth and the sun. This is the beginning of its monthly cycle and said to be a good time to set intentions as it is ripe with possibility. It's when the moon is at its darkest point because it is conjunct the sun and, thus, its reflection is blocked. This would be equivalent to the Water phase in the Five Elements Cycle, the phase in which you plant seeds of ideas and desires. It's when the veil is the thinnest between us and the spirit world. This is also associated with the time of menstruation for women's menstrual cycle, which also coordinates with the phases of the moon. With each day, the moon waxes, or increases, in size from crescent to half-moon. This is equivalent to the Wood phase, when energy gains momentum.

When the moon reaches its full moon position, exactly opposite the sun, it's in its most potent energy phase. We can feel its effects from oceanic tidal waves to emotional rollercoasters. Night court judges know to expect an unusually busy night when the moon is full. When the energy reaches this apex, this is equivalent to the Fire phase in the Five Elements Cycle. From this point, the moon begins to wane, which would be the Metal phase, and then completes the cycle by returning back to the new moon phase, the Water phase, where energy begins and ends. You could do the same analysis for your day, starting from when you wake up until you go to bed, or the year in terms of seasons. Our natural circadian rhythms are in sync with the Five Elements Cycle with the sun and moon being the primary yin and yang energy polarities. The same phases are the foundation for all activities and projects, including exercise and yoga practices.

Five Elements in Yoga

One of the most rewarding jobs I've ever had was teaching yoga. My favorite class was a vinyasa class that met after work and attracted stressed-out yogis needing to relax and also move their body after sitting at a desk all day. Like many yoga classes, I started out with a short centering meditation sitting cross-legged or in child's pose. This is the Water phase. From there, you start to warm the body up in the Wood phase, stretching out what feels like stiff tree trunks. A vinyasa-style yoga class typically moves into sun salutations, which are a series of poses used to build up heat in the body. Appropriately named after the sun, this is the Fire phase of the class. Most yoga classes incorporate balance postures, which would be the Earth phase. And then there is a cooldown period, the Metal phase, when more focus is put on precision and form.

Everything ends from where it begins—the Water phase. Like many yogis, this is my favorite phase of a yoga class. In ancient Sanskrit, it's called *savasana,* which translates to "corpse pose," to mimic death. In traditional yoga traditions, the movement poses are all for the purpose of preparing your mind and body to take a seat for meditation. The practice takes you full circle to end up where you began, only now in a heightened form of preparedness. This is the idea of the spiral, where we circle back around for the purpose of expansion rather than repetition.

Yoga philosophy, which is based in Vedic sciences from India, uses theories similar to Taoism, so it's no wonder that a typical asana practice would so closely resemble the Five Elements Cycle. However, it's not only Eastern-based practices that follow the Five Elements Cycle. If allotted enough time, most exercise regiments start with a warm-up bookended with a cooldown. It's natural for us to follow the sequence of the Five Elements, and when we don't, we're more prone to injuries. It's easy to want to skip steps in anything we do, whether it's to save time or because we underestimate its importance. Like me, you've probably skipped over the warm-up or cooldown phase before exercising or playing a sport only to later realize that was a mistake. The same thing happens in any endeavor, none more so than the process of writing.

Five Elements in Writing

My understanding of the Five Elements Cycle as the template for the creative process materialized from teaching the Five Elements to my feng shui students. The Five Elements are one of the most difficult concepts to teach and understand in feng shui because of the many cycles the elements go through, which are beyond the scope of this book. In searching for examples of the Five Elements Cycle, I borrowed from my experience of writing and publishing. Going from idea to completion of a manuscript is the perfect example of the Five Elements Cycle. I further realized that the Five Elements Cycle applied not only to writing but to any creative process because it *is* the creative process. Since then, I've used the Five Elements Method to help writers have context for where they are in the overall process that can otherwise feel overwhelming.

If you've ever attempted to write a book, then you know it's a long process. The numbers aren't on your side either. It's been speculated in the writing community that 97 percent of those who start writing a book don't finish it, which means only 3 percent of people who start writing a book actually complete it. Whether that number is accurate or not, the sentiment speaks volumes. When you break down the book writing process into the components of the Five Elements, you can quickly see where your project derailed and how to get it back on track. You'll find that the key is most likely connected to your missing element. In part 2, you'll discover what your missing element is so that you can overcome past challenges. For now, however, let's take a step-by-step look at the writing process through the lens of the Five Elements.

A book starts with an idea. You now know that the idea phase is the Water phase, where thoughts and ideas seem to come out of thin air. Although the phrase *thin air* is credited to Shakespeare in *The Tempest*, I think of the phrase as referring to when thoughts or ideas come from Spirit. This usually happens when we are in a relaxed state allowing for the veil between heaven and earth to be unobstructed and thus thinner. This could be a time of day or during a particular activity, such as meditation, showering, or sleeping.

From when or where do your best ideas or aha moments come to you? For me, they come when I'm literally immersed in the Water element in the shower or bath. Ideas also tend to come when I'm moving my feet in a steady motion, such as taking a walk or rollerblading. I find a meditation practice creates a conduit, or bridge, for ideas to flow through even if they're not transmitted in the moment. Ideas are more likely to come at random times throughout my day when I've meditated that morning. It's as if I've cleared a path for them to come in. Ideas or messages could also come from other people, even strangers, almost like messengers delivering you information from the divine. In chapter 10, we'll explore activities associated with the Water element for those wanting to access more Water energy.

The Water phase is also associated with knowing your *why*. In other words, what's driving you to write about or explore a certain topic. Your *why* becomes the river that quietly flows underneath your project and takes you to the end. It is what will get you past the doubts and fears along your journey. Your *why* may feel like your mission or purpose as it usually comes from a place bigger than ourselves. You will likely need to return to the Water phase throughout your project to remind yourself of your *why*. If it's a strong enough motivator, it will eventually win and get you through to the end. If you find yourself not moving beyond the Water phase, then check in with your *why* and determine whether it's strong enough at this time. For those with a lot of ideas for writing projects, it may be a matter of choosing the one with the strongest pulse. Once you have your *why*, it's now up to the other elements to help manifest it into physical form.

Everyone has good ideas that come and go, maybe even million-dollar ideas. However, they're worthless unless you do something with them. In other words, you must move the idea from the Water phase to the Wood phase. Our intellectual property laws even recognize this concept. Ideas must be put into a tangible form to have copyright protection. The second you write your idea down in any form, you own a copyright.

Congratulations! Our copyright laws are basically congressional legislation of the formalities of moving from the Water phase to the Wood phase.

In writing, you enter the Wood phase when you put pen to paper or fingers to keyboard to start writing out your idea. It could be as simple as jotting down your idea onto a napkin, creating an outline, or dictating notes for a story on your phone. Anything to get your thoughts into a tangible form. For nonfiction books, I start with creating an outline to put ideas into a logical book format. The outline changes slightly along the way, but I at least have a map of sorts to keep me on course.

Some writers are more akin to early pioneers who begin their journey without a map into the unknown. This approach can be effective for fiction or memoir writers who like to see where the adventure takes them or who prefer to use writing as a discovery process. For example, iconic writer Joan Didion wrote, "I write entirely to find out what I'm thinking, what I'm looking at, what I see and what it means. What I want and what I fear."[6] She uses writing as a self-reflection tool. In using this approach, the map is filled in later as a memory marker of where you went.

I remember the TripTik Travel Planner maps from AAA that my mom would have for our family vacations. Our route was highlighted with a yellow highlighter and planned to the exact gas station stop. No time was wasted on our trips, that's for sure. I suppose this planned approach rubbed off on me, as I too prefer to have a map to avoid too many bunny trails. That being said, I also appreciate staying open because detours are inevitable and spontaneity makes the trip much more interesting. The same is true for the writing journey.

Once you've created an outline, even if only a skeleton outline or a starting point, next up is the actual writing of the book.

This is the Fire phase. This phase is affectionally referred to as the "shitty first draft," a term coined by Anne Lamott in her best-selling book *Bird by Bird*.[7] The goal is to get your first draft down without worrying about how good it is or how many mistakes you've made. You just write from your heart. This is the embodiment of the Fire element, in which the output of energy is at its height. You set aside your perfectionistic inner critic, which is the shadow side of the Metal element, and write from your intuitive right brain. There will be plenty of time for the logical left brain when you get to the Metal phase.

In Chinese Medicine, the Fire element is represented by the heart. Simply put, it takes heart to crank out a full manuscript. You need to be passionate about what you're writing to get you through the many hours it takes. In *The Artist's Way*, Julia Cameron writes that "being an artist requires enthusiasm more than discipline." She calls it a "spiritual commitment, a loving surrender to our creative process, a loving recognition of all the creativity around us."[8] It's at this stage when you may need to return to the Water phase to remember your *why*. This is also a good reminder that the phases are not necessarily linear. The elements are interdependent on one another, and, thus, you may find yourself revisiting some of the phases along the way to finishing your project.

After you've finished your first draft, any writing teacher or coach is going to tell you to step away from it for a while. Let it marinate. You need a break from it so that you can return with fresh eyes. This is the Earth element phase of the writing process. In the Five Elements Cycle, the Fire element creates Earth in the same way volcano magma creates land masses. This is an important point of the writing process that's often overlooked. After you've had some days, weeks, months, or even years away from it, look back on it with a new perspective, but this time from the readers' perspective. If you're writing for commercial purposes, then it's a good time to ask yourself these questions: Who is your audience? Does your writing effectively communicate your message? What is your publishing goal? The answers to these questions will give useful insight into the next phase, the Metal element.

Once you've finished your first draft and have had time to reread it and reflect upon it, it's then time for the Metal element, when you go back and edit your first draft. Technically, this is your second draft. If you were true to the Fire phase, then you should have plenty to edit. The Fire doesn't worry about where its sparks land; it just burns bright for the moment. Some writers would love to be in this phase for their entire career. Who cares about editing or selling books? They love to crank out words. But often the gold is literally found in the Metal element phase. It's here where words are chosen with precision and the book starts to take shape and structure with more clarity and a sharper focus.

You can think of the Metal phase as the decluttering phase of your manuscript, in which you decide what's redundant, what's not needed, and what's taking away from the story or information. This is also the time to refine your chapter outline from the Wood element phase. In the Five Elements Cycle, Metal controls Wood, and, thus, anything that was not feasible from the Wood phase now gets cut out in the Metal phase. This is how nature maintains its sustainability. Imagine a book that was not edited. You would have to wade through pages and pages of irrelevant or useless words.

Once through the second draft, from here you can see if you need to go back to one of the other elements. Perhaps you realize you need to write more in a particular chapter. Maybe it needs more examples or more of your personal story in it. If this is the case, then you'll return to the Fire phase for more writing. Or maybe you need to remind yourself of your *why* in the Water phase to motivate you to go back into the Metal phase for one more round of editing.

Whether it's creating a book, a product, or a child, we are ultimately spiritual beings having a physical experience by turning thoughts into things through the creative process of the Five Elements. This is the reason I love creating books. My *why* behind writing this book is to help others with this process in anything they want to create. While creating a book epitomizes this process, so does the process of designing products, interior spaces, and architecture.

Five Elements in the Design Process

A few years into practicing law, I felt creatively stifled. Shuffling papers wasn't enough. I needed to be creating, I just didn't know what. And then, I started having dreams at night of interior spaces unlike anything I'd seen before. During that time, I met someone who was graduating from interior design school as his second career. This piqued my curiosity. And then I had a random encounter with a stranger at a bar one night. In response to my lamenting about how much I didn't want to practice law, this young man who was celebrating his twenty-first birthday asked me, "What do you dream about at night? I dream of flying, so I'm going to be a pilot." Could it be that easy? Life can be simple if we allow it to be. That next week I enrolled in interior design school at Watkins College of Art & Design, which had a night program. Unfortunately, the dreams stopped as soon as I started school, leaving me reliant upon my own imagination.

I was able to come up with some decent spaces, but it wasn't until I learned how to sketch perspective drawings when I hit my stride with the design process. I loved to imagine a space in my head and draw it rather accurately on paper. This art form was a valuable means of communication. Because we can't see other people's thoughts, we have to put them in a physical form in order to communicate them to our spouse, the contractor, or our clients. Even if not meant for commercial use, an art piece is an expression of feelings or thoughts that the artist has made tangible.

About three-fourths of the way through interior design school, I decided that I didn't want to be an interior designer after all. This was disheartening and caused me a lot of self-doubt since I had had such clear signs. I reluctantly finished out my degree and started a business generating hand-drawn and computer-generated renderings for designers, builders, and architects. I wanted to focus on the Wood element phase of the design process—the rest would be up to the Fire and Metal elements to implement the project from there. Soon thereafter, feng shui fell onto my path, and the yellow brick road that I could not have seen until then appeared before me.

Like seeing a designed space in my mind's eye, the idea or vision comes and must then get transposed into some tangible form, such as in a journal, on a computer, or on a cocktail napkin. Next, it's essential to create a prototype, blueprint, rendering, script, or mood board. Never would you go from idea to installation, unless you're really cutting corners. Have you ever ordered a couch without doing proper measurements only for it to show up way too big for your space? If so, you and many others skipped the Wood phase.

The next phase of the design process is the Fire element phase, when the building, sculpting, practicing, resourcing, purchasing aspects of the project take place. In other words, the majority of your energy. The Fire phase is the active, yang phase of the project when you put most of your time and energy into it. You give it your all here, perhaps even losing track of time or sleep. You'll catch up in the Earth phase when you crash after putting all your energy into the creating phase. In the Earth element phase, you'll also test out your design and get feedback and approvals from your client or anyone else involved in the process.

Once the bulk of the work is done, it's time to edit in the Metal element phase. What doesn't work? What distracts? What costs too much? What needs to be cut? In other words, what changes will make the product or design even better, similar to the second or third draft of a manuscript. The Metal phase puts that shiny polish on a project that makes it shine. This is an essential step for any successful design, and as you can imagine, it's also a crucial step for the success of making television and film, which we'll look at next in terms of the Five Elements Cycle.

Five Elements in Filmmaking

Going to the movies with my parents on Friday nights was one of my favorite things to do as a child. I knew I was a little different from my peers when in fifth grade a friend asked me what I did over the weekend and I said, "I saw *On Golden Pond*! It was so amazing!" I didn't get a lot of agreement in lunch line that day, but I did from the Academy as the film won Best Picture that year. Making movies is a process that I've been enamored with for years. I love when a group of people, all doing what they do best, come together to create a vision. Being part of a stage play has the same allure. Since living in Los Angeles, I've taken acting classes, producing classes, directing classes, and writing classes and played with the idea of set design. I've had enough experience in most sides of the prism to know that filmmaking is a grand orchestration of the Five Elements Cycle.

Whether it's a documentary, a short film, a TV episodic, or a feature film, it all starts with an idea in the Water phase. If there's already a script (that would have gone through its own Five Elements Cycle), then the next step would be to storyboard the scenes. This is equivalent to the map in the Wood element phase, along with all the pre-production steps of obtaining financing and securing legal contracts. The actual shooting of the film with the entire crew and actors on set would be the Fire element phase. This is the production phase, where, true to the Fire element, the momentum, the energy, and the passion of everyone involved continues until filming has completed. From there, the film goes into post-production, where it goes through editing. This is of course the Metal phase. The film is then wrapped up and released to begin a new Five Elements cycle into distribution and viewership. From there, a new movie is started in the Water phase because the show must go on.

Five Elements in Relationships

The Five Elements Cycle is the process of creating not only tangible things but anything of significant longevity, including a relationship. Think about when you met your significant other or someone important to you. It probably began with a desire to have a relationship. That desire is a super-powered thought called an emotion. This is the Water phase. From there, maybe you downloaded a dating app, or frequented places to make yourself more available, or confided in your friends in case they knew of someone who could be a match. In other words, you took action steps—the Wood phase. And then you met that person. Fireworks. Butterflies. Whatever it was, you felt something stir within you. You continued dating, getting serious, and fell in love. This is the Fire element phase.

Whether it's a project or a person, the Fire phase has an addictive quality because of the rush of energy we feel. Inevitably, however, the energy isn't sustainable. The relationship plateaus in the Earth element phase, you settle into a rhythm and feel comfortable with that person. And then what happens? The critiquing begins. The relationship enters the Metal phase. If you make it through this phase, then congratulations: it has potential to go the long haul. The relationship continues going around and around the Five Elements Cycle with new iterations of expansion each time. If you ever feel like you're repeating patterns in relationships, the truth is you are. However, each passing has the same qualities (and stories), but with more experience and wisdom with each go-around. This is the quality of the spiral that provides expansion that happens as we make our way through the Five Elements Cycle.

I've now walked you through some of my favorite interests—yoga, writing, design, filmmaking, and relationships—as examples of how the creative process of the Five Elements Cycle works. You can apply this same analysis to any activity in your life, including something as simple as getting together with a friend. There is the desire to get together followed by making the plan, the buildup, the excitement, the wrap-up, and the good-bye. Ultimately, the Five Elements Cycle is about expanding and enriching our world, but at a pace that's sustainable and not overwhelming. Each phase is essential for building upon the next, just like a relationship. You've likely heard sayings such as "the candle that burns twice as bright burns half as long" or "burning a candle at both ends," implying that the intensity of the fire won't last as long as that of a slow burn. This happens when a relationship goes directly to the Fire phase without any of the other elements supporting it. So too could it happen with a project.

Now that you understand how the cycle works, you're probably starting to notice which phase tends to hang you up. This phase is probably a weakness in multiple areas of your life because how we do one thing is how we do everything. You may also notice which phase is your favorite. For me, I love getting ideas in the Water phase and starting new projects in the Wood phase, but going all in and committing in the Fire phase is where I become challenged. I now use tools to stay focused to get through the Fire phase. This is exactly what you'll learn to do in part 2 for each of the elements.

In part 2, you'll become super clear on which phase is your strength and which phase is your weakness by determining your primary element and your missing element. Once you have this information, you will start to see why you've been successful at times and why certain projects stalled or never got off the ground. You'll fill in the gap to your own Five Elements Cycle and start mastering the creative process.

PART 2

Integrating the Five Elements within Yourself

CHAPTER 4
Determining Your Primary Element

Whatever the circumstances of your life, the understanding
of type can make your perceptions clearer, your judgments
sounder, and your life closer to your heart's desire.

—Isabel Briggs Myers

According to Taoism, we were all created from the same matter that makes up the Five Elements and, thus, all have the inherent qualities of all Five Elements within us. This is the same energy that creates stars, planets, and worlds and is the premise behind the spiritual tenet "We are all one." At the same time, we are each an individual being for the purpose of individuation through which creative energy finds expression. We are each an expression of Source energy with a unique perspective given our particular skills, talents, desires, and past experiences.

We each embody a different concentration of the elements. This is an approach used in Chinese Medicine for treating patients when an imbalance occurs. In Chinese Medicine, each organ system is associated with one of the Five Elements.[9] When the Five Elements are working harmoniously, we are in good health. When they're out of balance, Chinese Medicine practitioners will use acupuncture and herbal remedies, among other modalities, to rebalance the interrelationship of the elements in the body to bring about harmony and balance once again.

Psychological Use of the Five Elements

While we embody all Five Elements, we are also unique in the concentration of each element. For example, some people have more yang energy, embodying more Wood or Fire elements, while others are naturally more yin and thus embody more Metal or Water elements. This individual makeup of energy will play a role in one's physical characteristics, energy level, and even personality traits. Some people may have a high concentration in one element, while someone else may be more evenly balanced among all five elements. In other words, we each have our own Five Elements constitution that makes us unique.

In its original Taoist origins, the Five Elements were not viewed in terms of the individual until thousands of years later when Chinese Medicine applied the Five Elements for purposes of medical diagnoses. It was only after Chinese Medicine migrated to the West when the Five Element phases were also viewed as a system of typology for individual personality types.[10] While there is no historical marker for this migration, it most likely occurred as a result of the depth psychology movement spearheaded by psychoanalyst Carl Jung. Until then, the individual ego that gives rise to one's personality was not examined to the extent it is today.

Classical or traditional feng shui, also rooted in Chinese Medicine, is based on an earth-centric model that gives little, if any, consideration to the effect of humans in the space. As feng shui traveled West, the practice became more human-centric by emphasizing the power of the human mind. This mirrors the values of different cultures. Both views hold merit and represent

the yin-yang polarity on the planet. As Eastern and Western ideologies merge, we get to experience the best of both worlds. This
includes using the Taoist-based principles of the Five Elements as
a psychological tool to gain access to more self-awareness.

Personality tests are now "a roughly $500 million industry,
with an annual growth rate estimated at 10% to 15%."[11] According
to the *Harvard Business Review*, it's now common for employers to
require workers to take personality assessments "as part of their
personnel selection, to improve collaboration and teamwork, and
to identify satisfying career paths."[12] The Myers-Briggs Type Indi-
cator test was developed in the 1960s and has been considered the
most popular personality assessment test to date. Even though it
gained popularity in the workplace, the Myers-Briggs test origi-
nated when Katharine Briggs began researching personality to
"understand what she saw as an unlikely attraction" between her
daughter and her daughter's fiancé.[13]

Considering that the field of psychology was developed only
150 years ago and only became mainstream approximately fifty
years ago, we've had a relatively short amount of time in our evolution to consider who we are, what we want, and what makes
us happy. We also have more options than ever in choosing what
career or relationship is best for us, particularly for women who
were historically exempt from such choices. It's now rare to commit to one career or one person and stick with it for the rest of
our life. The pursuit of what will make us happy is not as easy
as it seems and takes self-inquiry to help find what will bring us
satisfaction. Perhaps this is an indication of graduating beyond the
grips of survival, or at least a higher level of consciousness that we
can now access.

While no personality assessment test can give us all the answers we seek, a test can be a helpful guidepost for who we are compared to the other billions of people in the world. Our ego wants to know that we belong, but it also wants to be different so that we can feel special, but not too special because then we won't belong. Did you follow that? The point is, pleasing the ego is an empty bucket of insecurities.

Knowing that we fit into a category can be comforting, but it can also be limiting to the full breadth of who we are and who we can become. What's unique about the Five Elements Quiz is that we're all made up of all Five Element personality types. The difference is in the concentration of each of the elements that makes me different from you. At our base, we all share these core energies. Our individuality is expressed with each one of us having a slightly different concentration of each element. In other words, we all have the same recipe, just a different amount of each ingredient. And it's an ongoing, everchanging recipe, not a one-time meal. Your profile may change as you go through different phases and experiences throughout your life.

Your Five Elements Profile

Hopefully, by now your ego is eager to know which category it fits into, while your higher self is ready to embody all Five Elements. By simply reading the elemental descriptions in chapter 2, you probably already have a good idea which elements you are stronger and weaker in. Usually, there are one or two elements that feel natural to us and at least one element that feels foreign or challenging. Knowing our strengths and weaknesses is invaluable to knowing how to navigate them in work and relationships.

We generally gravitate to tasks or activities that come easier, while avoiding those that are difficult. Inevitably, however, we run into situations when we have to step into a role in which we have to use our weak element. Maybe you're involved with a nonprofit organization and then out of the blue you're asked to speak at one of their meetings. Or you're a creative who wants to turn your art into a business, but you know nothing about running a business. Knowing your weak element can help guide you to know when it's best to hire or partner with someone versus doing it yourself.

It's important to note that there is no element constitution that's better than another. For example, some people come into the world with a high concentration of one of the elements to carry out a specific life purpose. Other people are well-rounded, jack-of-all-trade types that have an equal familiarity with all or several of the elemental energies for their purpose. The goal is not to score even among all the elements, nor is it to change who you are, but to maximize your potential.

It's not uncommon to have a tie of two or more elements for your primary element or your missing element. It is common to have a tie of Wood and Fire for your primary element or Water and Metal, which shows that you are more dominant in yang energy or yin energy, respectively. In the following quiz, if you have a tie of elements with opposing energies, such as Water and Fire or Wood and Metal, then you have an internal balancing mechanism of yin and yang energies.

Either way, I encourage you to read the description of the elements in which you tied in the next chapter and notice which description sounds most like you. Sometimes we can recognize our traits through a narrative description more than through taking a quiz. If both elemental descriptions sound 100 percent like you, then there is no problem to having a primary element in more than one element.

In the case of a tie for your missing element, I also recommend reviewing the descriptions in the next chapter. From there, you will likely notice that one of the elements in which you scored a tie is the least like you. That is your missing element. If more than one of the descriptions sounds like your missing element, then you might consider which element you would most want to cultivate or focus on at this time in your life.

After you take the following quiz to determine your Five Elements profile, you'll know your baseline constitution. That is who you are at your core before you start applying new focus and energy on elements you might not otherwise use on a regular basis. In other words, you have dormant energies within you that can unlock new aspects of yourself. In the successive chapters, you'll start to embrace and integrate your weaker, or missing, element to awaken all Five Elements within you.

Over the evolution of our life, we cycle through the five phases with our life span being the overarching cycle. Underneath the umbrella of our life span, we experience many mini cycles throughout our lives based on our astrology, our choices, and collective influences. As we grow and evolve, we also embody more of our Self, our own energy, our pure essence, which is a full expression of creation and the creative cycle. This includes embodying more of the elements within.

With age comes wisdom because we have experienced more of these Five Element phases throughout our life span. We've lived through grief, we've lived through letting go, we've lived through celebrations, youth, and aging. We've lived through multiple spirals of the Five Elements Cycle. Perhaps that's why a young child resists the transition of leaving the park when it's time to go. The experience of letting go and endings, the energy of the Metal phase, is a foreign concept. The child hasn't yet learned that life gives you more opportunities to experience it again.

The Five Elements Quiz uses a questionnaire that gives you room to be who you are now without a static label you carry with you for the rest of your life. As you change, your answers may change, but most will stay consistent for the majority of your life. The quiz will give you an accurate Five Elements profile for this point in time. You can always come back to it in the future to see how you've changed. The quiz will show you how you rank among all Five Elements, from highest to lowest. Take a few moments to determine your Five Elements profile, followed by an in-depth description of each of the element types in the subsequent chapters.

Five Elements Quiz

For each statement, score yourself using the following:

2 = Very much like me

1 = Sometimes like me

0 = Not me at all

Group A Questions

_____ People would say I'm shy or quiet.

_____ I don't set goals because you never know where life will take you.

_____ I can easily get lost in my own world.

_____ I would rather stay at home with a good book than attend a social event.

_____ People don't really know me outside my inner circle and I'm good with that.

_____ **Group A Score**

Group B Questions

_____ I love starting new projects and often have multiple going at the same time.

_____ I'm often on the cutting edge in my work and love learning new things.

_____ I'm good at making decisions and take action on them rather quickly.

_____ People see me as a leader.

_____ I get frustrated when things don't happen fast enough.

_____ **Group B Score**

Group C Questions

_____ I'm a better speaker than writer, but I enjoy all forms of communication.

_____ When I'm passionate about a project, I'm all in and can almost become obsessed with it.

_____ I am generally a people person and enjoy the company of others.

_____ I am affectionate.

_____ At times, I exhaust myself to the point of crashing.

_____ **Group C Score**

Group D Questions

_____ I don't make a lot of changes, but when I do, they're pretty major.

_____ In social or family groups, I tend to be the glue that keeps everyone together.

_____ I'm very supportive of other people's goals and will even go out of my way to help.

_____ I'm more likely to go along with the group than assert my opinion and upset people.

_____ My friends often lean on me for advice and support.

_____ **Group D Score**

Group E Questions

_____ I tell people the truth without BS or embellishments.

_____ I maintain a neat and orderly environment without too much clutter.

_____ I am self-disciplined.

_____ I prefer an analytical approach to problem-solving rather than relying on feelings.

_____ I like to keep things organized.

_____ **Group E Score**

All Group Scores

_____ Group A Score = Water Element

_____ Group B Score = Wood Element

_____ Group C Score = Fire Element

_____ Group D Score = Earth Element

_____ Group E Score = Metal Element

Your Five Elements Profile

From your scores, make a list of your elements from highest score to lowest score. This is your personal Five Elements Profile. It's the energetic recipe that makes you *you*. Next up, get to know each of these aspects within yourself that are available to you anytime.

#1 _____   ← **Your Primary Element**

#2 _____

#3 _____

#4 _____

#5 _____   ← **Your Missing Element**

CHAPTER 5

Getting to Know Your Personal Board of Directors

> Be really whole,
> And all things will come to you.
> —*Tao Te Ching*, translated by
> Gia-fu Feng and Jane English

If you're a solo practitioner or single-owner company, like myself, then you've most likely had to wear many hats, from marketing manager to money manager and everything in between. Until you hire employees or start a corporation with a full board of directors, you're in the position of CEOE—chief executive officer of everything. The good news is that you are completely qualified for this position. In fact, by the time you get to know your board of directors, you might be so impressed that you realize it's time to give your CEOE a raise. If you're wanting to start a business, the Five Elements provide the perfect template for the skillsets needed. If you work for a corporation, then getting to know your personal board of directors will show you where you can best contribute and how to raise the bar for more opportunities. Perhaps it's time for your office in the C-suite.

You now have your Five Elements Profile and know how you rank among all the elements. You've also identified your *primary element* and your *missing element*. Your primary element is an energy you're familiar with and is already well-integrated. In the descriptions that follow for each element, you'll immediately recognize yourself in the character traits of your primary element. As previously mentioned, it's possible that you had two high-scoring elements that tied as your primary element or missing element. As you read the descriptions of the character traits for each element, you'll likely be able to narrow it down to one primary element and one missing element. If not, that's okay. You're simply multifaceted and already on your way to embracing all five elements.

Your profile is specific to you and is what makes you unique. You can now gain insight into your current energetic patterns, as well as those aspects with which you might not be as familiar. You'll find that some of the elements are naturally more accessible to you than others, but all can be learned, integrated, and used when needed. Think of each element taking a seat at the board of directors' table with its unique talents and learned skillsets to whom you can call on at any time.

In the following sections, you'll get to know each element acting individually as an officer and operating together as your board of directors to run your Fortune 500 company called You, Inc. Your primary element will be the most noticeable, as it's the board member who always shows up to vote, but also give attention to the description of your missing element. The character description will probably read like a foreign language. It will probably sound nothing like you. However, the description likely contains traits you've expressed a desire or need to embrace but that seemed out of reach.

As you read through the descriptions for the elements, start putting in your order for qualities you'd like to embody more or perhaps less. Your board is made up of your inner guru, leader, motivator, stabilizer, and organizer. How can you make more use of your board of directors? Once you have the awareness and understanding of who's available, you'll then learn how to integrate each of these elements into your daily life for more accessibility when needed. Let's start with your inner guru, who's necessary to bring wisdom to any project or situation.

The Water Element: Your Inner Guru

Imagine having someone who you can always turn to at a moment's notice to provide you with wise counsel. Perhaps you have someone in your life whom you can trust to give you good advice, such as a parent, best friend, spiritual advisor, or therapist. If you do, consider yourself fortunate. Mentors come and go throughout our life as we need them. A common saying among spiritual traditions is that when the student is ready, the teacher will appear. There are times along our journey when we're forced to go it alone. In context of the hero's journey, our mentors and allies fall away as we cross the threshold and enter the dark night of the soul all alone. In these times, we must lean on our inner guru, the Water element. Of course, it's not only in times of crisis when we look to our Water element. It can be a reservoir of self-care, aha moments, and the portal to our spiritual home.

The Water element is the most yin, or passive, of all the elements, but do not underestimate this potent energy. It is the seed point for all creations. Anytime we seek solitude or alone time, we tap into our inner Water element to reconnect with Source energy. This allows us to become still, intuitive, introspective, and feel more connected to God, Spirit, or universal energy. When we have insight that seemingly comes from nowhere, it's the result of having taken time in the Water phase. Instead of dispersing our energy in the Wood and Fire phase, we go inward for rest and renewal. This is challenging for those with high energy, but not so for those with their primary element in Water. It is through quiet reflection that the Water element gathers its strength for the seasons ahead. The Water element embodies an inner beauty and quiet strength that is accessible and necessary for everyone.

Water Element as Your Primary Element

If Water is your primary element, then you are a quiet, introverted person on the exterior. People might underestimate you because your unassuming power comes through a quiet strength. You are deeply creative, contemplative, sensitive, and introspective with a rich interior world. Others may view you as withdrawn, even aloof at times. You keep your emotions close to you without revealing too much to those outside your inner circle. You take time to process information and are relatively calm in stressful situations. You have a deep reservoir of faith, and others may come to you for your wisdom and inspiration. You have strong intuition that you rely on and can trust. Your ideal weekend is being home reading, journaling, listening to music, and perhaps engaging in a creative project. In social situations, you prefer one-on-one deep discussions and find it challenging to talk about surface issues.

Primary Water Element at Work

You can often find Water elements at work as a writer, poet, researcher, librarian, painter, intuitive, healer, life coach, artist, dancer, healthcare provider, songwriter, therapist, or counselor. Water elements are brimming with original ideas but sometimes find it challenging to bring them to fruition. Because they feel more connected to the spiritual world than the physical realm, they can be challenged by money.

Water elements tend to live minimally without the need for extravagance and thus usually don't pursue a career for financial gravitas. Money is not what motivates them so much as being creative and being of service to the world in some way. Water elements may become known for their unique perspectives or new ways of seeing or living in the world. However, the challenge is making their work visible and accessible for distribution in a mainstream market.

In the workplace, the Water element is the one who sits in the back of meetings without anyone noticing them despite the fact that they hold the solution to the problem at hand. Partnering with Wood and Fire elements can assist the Water element in this process and bring more satisfaction to their work and life. It's important for them to protect their intellectual property and to not give all their best ideas away as work for hire.

Primary Water Element in Relationships

Of all the elements, the Water element is the most self-sufficient and at peace being alone. Because of their rich inner world and connection to Source, they are never bored. They seek fulfillment within, instead of looking outside of themselves. However, they do enjoy the company of intimate relationships, particularly with those who share similar ideologies and creative energy.

Water elements can expand their world through partnerships, particularly with Wood and Fire elements. The social demands of the Fire element may need to be negotiated, but they also provide a welcome break from living too much in their head. They generally find an easy compatibility with Wood and Metal. Earth elements may be a bit too clingy. After all, who needs to join a book club when you can sink into your own couch with a good book and glass of wine?

Too Much Water

Yes, it's possible to have too much of a good thing. Too much of any one element can lead to an imbalance when it goes beyond one's own constitution, which can happen in stressful times. There are telltale signs of an overbalance for each element. If your primary element is the Water element, then be aware if you start drowning in too much Water, which can lead to lethargy, depression, and an overall lack of motivation. An imbalance of the Water element can also show up as a fear of visibility. This can be particularly detrimental for artists and creatives who shy away from the spotlight because it can lead them further into isolation. Water elements are more comfortable in the spiritual world to the point where the physical world can feel overwhelming at times. While Water elements enjoy solitude, too much time alone can be unhealthy, as the mind can wander them down a dark road, finding it difficult to come back.

Some Water types may be considered a bit eccentric due to the amount of time they spend alone. It's important that they have outlets to activities or people to give them adequate energy and ties to the physical world. Incorporating more Wood and Fire energy can help overcome the low energy that can result with too much Water. A quick fix is using light therapy, particularly exposure to the sun, if available. Taking a walk or involving more movement in one's daily routine can help stimulate more Wood energy, along with other suggestions in chapters 8 and 9.

The Wood Element: Your Inner Leader

Without the initiating energy of the Wood element, we would not be alive. It's the Wood energy that escorted each of us through the birth canal when we were born and out of bed this morning. It's saying yes to this big world even if done so hesitantly. It's the energy that gives us the spirit of the pioneer to do new things. We are all a hero or heroine on our own hero's journey through life with our inner Wood element leading the way.

The Wood element takes the vision from the Water phase and adds the practical steps to bring it into physical reality by developing a plan. Being flexible and open to change is essential to the success of the Wood phase. These are the qualities that make a successful leader. Once the kinks are worked out, the Wood element is off to the races, where it can manifest to its highest potential before then transforming into the Fire element phase.

The Wood element is best symbolized as a tree that weathers a storm. The tree branches must bend, but not break. This is accomplished when it has a strong foundation from the grounding Earth element and nourishing Metal element. The Wood element can't do it alone, nor can any of the elements. All do their job in reliance on the others.

Wood Element as Your Primary Element

If the Wood element is your primary element, then you're a natural leader. You take the lead with groups, whether social, family, or work and create the necessary steps to get projects or activities off the ground and moving. You consider yourself to be both an introvert and extrovert. You are flexible. You are always learning new things and are quick to implement your ideas.

You are both intuitive and analytical in your approach. It takes both head and heart to invent the wheel, which you're ready and willing to do. Adaptability is key for success, as is the acceptance of failure, followed by the perseverance of continuing to move forward. Because you bore easily, you often have multiple projects going on at once. Your challenge is staying the course to see a project through to its end. If you're not moving forward in some way, you can become frustrated. When this happens, it's best to take a step back to re-evaluate the best course of action by setting a stronger foundation or a better map with which to navigate forward.

Primary Wood Element at Work

Wood elements make great CEOs, directors, authors, speakers, coaches, project managers, and teachers and are great in any career where you are leading, teaching, creating, or sharing information. They are best in work that engages the left and right brain. Wood elements work well with others, but they also enjoy their independence and often find themselves the lone wolf on projects. They love the idea of collaboration. However, they also struggle with it. They're so used to thinking outside the box and only seeing their point of view that it can be challenging to open it up for others' input. It's nevertheless important for Wood elements to get outside opinions to help tweak or improve their existing idea.

When work endeavors are not moving forward fast enough or roadblocks show up unexpectantly, it's a sign to pause and reassess. Like a pioneer discovering a new world, you may have to redraw your map or take a different path. Consider using your natural abilities to delegate in order to maintain your multiple projects or, in your case, manage multiple businesses simultaneously.

The Wood element feels best when on the move, whether it's running to meetings around town or hiking the Pacific Crest Trail. Sitting at a desk for long periods of time can be challenging for Wood elements, unless they're in the throes of starting a new project.

Primary Wood Element in Relationships

Like with a work project, the Wood element is likely to jump into a relationship full steam and figure out the details later. Wood elements love falling in love but can lose momentum when the newness wears off. However, they do make great partners because they are content with being alone or in a relationship and therefore don't require too much attention. They're best partnered with someone who, like themselves, enjoys ambition, spontaneity, and a desire for adventure.

Wood elements partner well with Fire elements who can add that spark of motivation to help them manifest their goals. The Wood element may find Earth elements to be hovering and controlling, while Metal elements cut into its grand plans. However, both elements play a role in the expansive nature of the Wood element by providing grounding and precision to the Wood element's ideas. Often, our best teachers are disguised as those who challenge us the most, and this is no exception for the Wood element.

Too Much Wood

Because the elements work as a cycle and are thus interdependent on the other, when one is out of balance, it affects the overall balance of the cycle. Therefore, if you are overbalanced in one element, then you will be underbalanced in another. This tendency is heightened during stress when we default to what we know the most. When this happens, we tend to become overbalanced in our primary element and underbalanced in our missing element. When we are balanced in our own constitution, we are in harmony. It's when stress overtakes us that our energy shifts out of alignment with our core constitution.

When the Wood element person is in balance, she keeps things moving forward and helps the world to do so as well by taking positive, steady steps. However, when one is overbalanced in the Wood element, there can be an attempt to expand too quickly without adequate support. Setbacks can happen as a result, which leads to frustration—an emotion all too common for Wood element people. The key for those dominant in the Wood element is to know that roadblocks and detours are inevitable. The kneejerk reaction may be to give up the project altogether. Instead, staying the course may be the more appropriate response by making tweaks where necessary. When you are a leader and often inventing the wheel, adaptability is paramount, as is following your inner guide. See setbacks as resets for something better. When it's time to take a step back, it's a sign to go back into the Water, find more grounding with the Earth element, or look to the Metal element for edits.

What's underneath the ground is as important as what we can visibly see above ground. If a tree is not adequately grounded, its growth will be stalled or even knocked over during a storm. In times of instability, it's best for the Wood element to integrate more of the Earth element, even if that means taking a break from the action. Otherwise, the Wood element will begin to take on Fire element qualities and the wood will get burnt. As a primary Wood element myself, this is a lesson I've had to learn. It's better to take a day off rather than spin your wheels busying yourself. Or better yet, take a vacation.

The Fire Element: Your Inner Motivator

While the Wood element gets the energy moving out of the Water phase, the Fire element picks up where it leaves off to bring the energy to its highest expression. To do this, the Fire element adds that spark of energy necessary to see projects to their highest potential. Fire elements are in essence a catalyst to help make existing ideas bigger. Call on the Fire element when you need to access your inner motivator. The Fire element contains the magic ingredient necessary for any successful project: enthusiasm.

In Chinese Medicine, the Fire element is ruled by the heart. This makes sense with the Fire element being full of warmth, passion, compassion, and excitement. They lead from the heart more than the head and are thus highly intuitive when they're in their flow. Because the heart emits more electromagnetic energy than any other area in the body, it acts as a giant magnet attracting to us our desires. This makes the Fire element a powerful manifester. You could get away with riding the Wood element through a project, but the project will not meet its highest potential without entering the Fire phase, where you put your passion into it. It's here where we have an opportunity to raise the bar of what we're capable of creating.

Fire Element as Your Primary Element

If the Fire element is your primary element, then people are drawn to your charm, your enthusiasm, and passion toward life. You're an extrovert and enjoy the company of others. Fire elements shine their light into the world to help people connect, laugh, and experience more joy. However, if you give too much of your energy away, which you often do, then you'll burn out. After all, you are a flame that attracts those who need more energy. With an abundant supply of energy, you can be challenged with knowing where to put your focus. But when you do, you can create anything. When you don't, you become scattered and eventually anxious.

Primary Fire Element at Work

Fire elements do well in careers in which they deal directly with people, including sales, social influencing, coaching, marketing, sports, performance, publicity, and public speaking. They have the drive to do well on their own as a solo entrepreneur so long as they have regular interactions with clients, customers, an audience, or a team of people. Others will be drawn to partner with Fire elements with their challenge being able to draw boundaries, knowing when an opportunity is and isn't in your best interest.

Fire elements should be mindful of how much they commit to and put on their plate. They have lots of energy to give but also have their own limits. Too many commitments will disperse the Fire element's energy and they will start to lose their shine. In extreme cases, their light turns in on itself, which can lead to depression. They can quickly flip the switch back on by eliminating things they've committed to and being okay saying no. It's also important for Fire elements to balance their time with adequate exercise for excess mental and physical energy.

Primary Fire Element in Relationships

Fire elements enjoy being in relationships. They are passionate and affectionate lovers—that is, unless they've given all their energy away to others. When this happens, the Fire element may need to retreat into her cave for a few days only to reemerge with a new sense of vitality. Fire elements pair well with Water elements as they provide the calm that helps bring them balance. This is also true with Metal elements as they help the Fire element focus their energy for best success. In some cases, the Fire element could find the Water element a rain on its parade and the Metal element a drain on its energy. Fire elements find easy compatibility with Wood and Earth elements.

Too Much Fire

Despite them being wildly popular by the other kids, I never cared for sparklers on the Fourth of July. Was I the only one who thought the sparks hitting your hand was uncomfortable? In truth, all fireworks made me nervous when lit by dads who were looking for cool points from their kid and other parents. The sparks that splay in all directions is the way a Fire element person becomes when out of balance. Instead of a laser, the energy mimics that of a sparkler or a misdirected Roman candle firework. When Fire elements take on too much and spread their energy too thin, they become scattered and unfocused which leads to overwhelm. This can have physical repercussions over time in the form of anxiety, anger, sleep issues, and possibly heart issues. It's also important that Fire elements get enough sleep to counterbalance the exertion of energy throughout the day.

Whether the Fire element is your primary element or not, we're all prone to overexerting ourselves in a culture where nothing ever seems to be enough. We all go through periods when we need the Fire element and other times when we've exhausted our inner fire. Being around people can stimulate us but also overstimulate us. These extremes are especially true for Fire elements because they are super sensitive to other people's energy. While they are extroverts, they can also be people pleasers, which exhausts them. It's therefore important that they balance their time with people with time in nature or time alone.

The Earth Element: Your Inner Stabilizer

The Earth element provides the proper grounding and stabilizing energy we need for any project or endeavor. Earth elements provide the stage, or the container, on which all the other elements get to express themselves. They act behind the scenes with no need for credit or visibility. Their repayment is the gratification of having all their people close by and, better yet, under their control. This way they feel safe and can smooth over anything that could rock the boat.

Earth elements' nemesis is change. The flip side of this, however, is that you can always count on an Earth element in rough times. They are there to lend a shoulder, ear, or helpful hand to keep things stabilized. Of course, change is inevitable. When an Earth element realizes this and makes a voluntary change, you can count on it being a major change with full follow-through. They will never act on a whim or make spontaneous choices. Instead, they take their time and put much thought into making a decision before taking action.

Earth Element as Your Primary Element

If the Earth element is your primary element, then you are the grounding force that helps maintain the status quo. You keep things stable so that change doesn't happen too quickly. You are a highly supportive person to others and help bring and maintain harmony among people, individually and in groups. People come to you for your support or a shoulder to lean on. You hold space for others' emotions, sometimes at the expense of your own. You do not like conflict and may even be conflict avoidant at times. You are a salt-of-the-earth-type person and get along with most people. You tell good stories.

You handle your finances well, but also tend to worry about money even if there's plenty. When you relax around money, you have the potential to reap quite a bountiful harvest. You do not like change and can worry if you sense change on the horizon. Your challenge is to not become controlling of situations that could lead to possible changes that are necessary for the growth of others and, of course, your own growth.

Primary Earth Element at Work

The Earth element is the quintessential team player and will often put the needs of others before their own. They have the nurturing qualities of a mother and can intuit the needs of others. This makes the Earth element great at any service-oriented career role, including teacher, healer, financial planner, chef or caterer, healthcare provider, counselor, humanitarian, or lawyer.

In groups, Earth elements are great at providing nonjudgmental feedback and pitching in when needed. They bring peace and harmony to groups. Being an amenable team player may even become part of their role or identity. Because of this, they're more likely to work with others rather than on their own. Earth elements are essential to the team, but may not always get the recognition they deserve, and certainly not the spotlight. They may even be willing to take one for the team, if necessary, and often sacrifice their desires for others, if it can help maintain harmony in groups.

Primary Earth Element in Relationships

Being in a relationship, particularly a marriage and family unit, constitutes a significant part of the Earth element's identity. In fact, being alone for too long is uncomfortable, unless it's become their own comfortable status quo. The Earth element is a loyal and supportive partner in love relationships. Codependence is the biggest challenge for Earth elements, as they tend to put others needs ahead of their own. Taking care of others and maintaining peace are familiar defaults for the Earth element. It's important for the Earth element to not give up their dreams at the expense of their partner's aspirations, as this could lead to resentment down the road.

Earth elements are the ultimate nurturers, using food and a safe sense of home as their love language. They partner well with Fire and Metal elements. Wood elements may challenge them beyond their comfort zone, while independent Water elements may not provide the level of day-to-day engagement the Earth element desires.

Too Much Earth

The grounding energy that Earth elements provide is their gift, but it can also lead to their detriment if they dig their heels so far into the ground that movement is impossible. Those with an imbalance of too much Earth will often avoid change to the point where change must happen to them rather than them feeling like they have power over their own life. Regardless of your primary element, there are times when we've all been too stubborn for our own good. If an Earth element puts off taking action for too long, it can lead to self-doubt disguised as procrastination.

Another sign of too much Earth is feeling worried about impending change. We all have a fear of the future to some extent, especially after the traumas experienced in 2020, but worrying for the sake of worrying can lead to control behaviors, lack of sleep, and exhaustion. Another symptom of too much Earth is enabling friends and partners with codependent behaviors. It's a common subconscious pattern to shape-shift into who others want us to be to keep the relationship going. However, this inevitably leads to resentment, upsets, and living inauthentically.

An overbalance of the Earth element can also lead to too much caretaking of others. The Earth element is the quintessential nurturer and the archetype of the mother. However, it's not always clear where love ends and caretaking begins in relationships with loved ones. The proverbial advice of putting your oxygen mask on first before helping others couldn't be truer for the Earth element. In taking care of everyone else, the Earth element neglects itself in the process.

Because the Earth element is the most grounded and, as its name implies, close to the earth, too much Earth energy can lead to an excess of physical items. Earth elements can literally get weighted down with belongings to the point where moving residences becomes an overwhelming feat. This can keep them locked into their current situation, for better or for worse, to the point of feeling stuck or even trapped. It's also not uncommon for Earth elements to become the dumping ground of inherited items from family members. This can eventually lead to emotions of overwhelm, resentment, and regret, with which they will cling to as well.

In the case of too much Earth, add more Wood and Fire energy to your life to stimulate forward-moving energy. The alternative would be to surrender into the Metal element and start the process of letting go of the density that has accumulated. If you need incentive, then begin dreaming and scheming in the Water phase what changes you'd like to see in your life. Create a vision so that you have incentive for letting go of the past. Visioning and taking action with decluttering are guaranteed antidotes to feeling stuck.

The Metal Element: Your Inner Organizer

Once a project has the stable grounding and reflection it needs, it's then up to the Metal element to extract anything in excess from the Fire phase that's not needed. Instead of adding or emitting energy into the world, the Metal element extracts energy as it passes through this phase of the Five Elements Cycle. You can think of the Metal element as the ultimate organizer or declutterer. They're able to sift through things, eliminate what's not needed, and leave only the best at the end. While the Earth element holds on to things, the Metal element is the master of letting go. Metal types remove the excess so that the best versions of everyone else's efforts can come forward. As energy decreases from what would otherwise be stagnation from the Earth cycle, a more refined and ordered version results. To accomplish this, the Metal element is extremely detailed and focused. They use systems and analysis over intuition. Like a good editor, their work is often overlooked. And because they are typically quiet introverts, you won't hear them toot their own horn.

Metal Element as Your Primary Element

If the Metal element is your primary element, then you are a natural organizer and keep things in check and on schedule. You are detail-oriented, focused, and precise in anything you do, from shopping to communicating. You cut to the chase in conversation without the need for embellishments. When you speak, people listen because of your direct communication style. You also have an orderly environment without much excess. You are efficient in anything you do, which makes you great at completing tasks. Your challenge is being obsessive-compulsive over little things and being a perfectionist. While you have the ability to focus, you may be challenged with seeing the big picture. If you become too narrow-minded, take a step back to see more of the forest and less of the trees.

Primary Metal Element at Work

If someone wants something done right, they ask a Metal element to do it. Metal elements are the taskmaster who knows how to complete a to-do list with quality and efficiency. They're on time and help others stay on schedule and organized. Metal elements make great architects, engineers, graphic designers, fashion designers, professional organizers, decorators, technical writers, scientists, accountants, athletes (in sports requiring precision, such as tennis, basketball, etc.), editors, critics, producers, classical musicians, and personal assistants. They are great with vocations that require tools, including scissors, a keyboard, measuring tape, a camera, machinery, plyers, or software. Metal elements prefer working alone, but they appreciate when their efforts contribute to something larger.

Primary Metal Element in Relationships

Metal elements are the least likely to seek out relationships and often prefer a more solitary lifestyle. They can have a *less is more* attitude that can apply to not only things but people too. When they do partner, it's often with someone who is very opposite from them, giving them the necessary challenge for growth, or someone who is equally independent. Metal elements keep an orderly home with their feathers easily ruffled if they live with someone who is messy or cluttered. This can sometimes lead to friction within their relationships.

Metal elements are drawn to minimalism with excess being a trigger for them. This is the exact reason they may be attracted to Wood or Fire elements in order to bring about balance to their otherwise sparse world. They find more ease and compatibility with the Water element who doesn't threaten their comfort zone. However, they may be attracted to those who create the spark they secretly desire.

Too Much Metal

In the case of an overbalance of the Metal element, people can become obsessive, controlling, perfectionistic, critical, or overly rigid in their thinking. Because of their attention to detail, they can become particular about their immediate environment to the point of being difficult to live with because of their need for an impeccably neat and controlled space. An overbalance of Metal starts in the mind with being closed- or narrow-minded, and this will eventually show up in their physical body as being rigid, inordinately thin or frail, and prone to allergies.

With an overbalance of the Metal element, one can also come across as critical to others, but also critical with themselves through negative self-talk. Because the Metal element relies on analytical thinking first, people with this dominant element can often ignore or deny their intuition to their detriment. In the case of too much Metal, it would be best to engage with Wood or Fire activities or people to help burn through some of the extreme tendencies.

Your Board of Directors in Action

The following figure provides a snapshot of your board of directors that you can call on anytime. You are multidimensional in who you are and what you can accomplish. Of course, I'm not suggesting that we be everything to everyone or need to master each of these elements evenly across the board. Instead, we can call on these aspects of ourselves with more intentionality when needed. We can also call on others to fill in these missing elements when needed. Recognizing these essential phases or steps of the creative process and how your strengths and challenges play into the cycle is groundbreaking in how you approach solo projects and collaborations going forward.

You now have awareness of the element and phase of the creative process with which you struggle, based upon your missing element. This phase has likely tripped you up time after time, prevented you from finishing, or even starting, something in the past that was important to you. Each phase is essential. It's now time to embrace the element you've avoided, until now. It may be the missing piece that you didn't know you needed and could bring you the treasure you've been seeking.

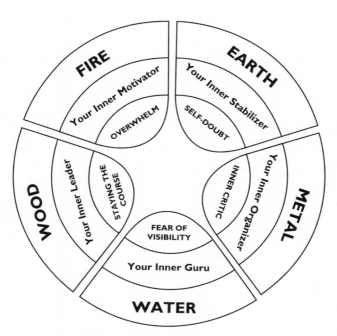

Figure 3. The Five Elements as Personality Types

CHAPTER 6

Transforming Your Missing Element into Your Hidden Strength

> Perhaps all the dragons in our lives are princesses who are only
> waiting to see us act, just once, with beauty and courage.
> Perhaps everything that frightens us is, in its deepest essence,
> something helpless that wants our love.
>
> —Rainer Maria Rilke

When I worked with clients' homes, I would sometimes notice a room or area of the house that wasn't like the others. It was usually an area of their home they ignored, didn't like, or to which they kept the door closed. It's easy to think that out of sight is out of mind, but our subconscious is always aware of everything. One client in particular kept a spare room locked, not because it contained valuables but because it was where she stored items she didn't want to deal with following her divorce. According to feng shui principles, it was in the "love corner" of her home. This locked room represented her heart that was closed off to love after being hurt.

When I come across a room or area that stands out from the rest of the home in a not-so-flattering way, I get excited because this area shows me where this client can make major changes in their life. It represents the area of this person's life that is ripe for transformation. In the example, she was ready to open back up to love by unlocking the room and dealing with the past. When we identify a challenging area in our home, then we've identified a correlating challenging area within ourselves too. As we make changes in a particular area of the home, a positive ripple effect occurs in our life.

We can also do this by identifying aspects within ourselves to which we've closed the door. Another word for these missing aspects is our *shadows*, a term coined by psychoanalyst Carl Jung, meaning those parts of ourselves that we abandoned years ago out of survival. Jung's career centered around the importance of integrating our shadows to become more whole and to live a more conscious life for our soul's expansion and our personal satisfaction in life. In *The Middle Passage: From Misery to Meaning in Midlife*, author James Hollis expands on the work of Carl Jung to explore how we can reclaim those lost parts of ourselves because "it is the only way to bring some balance back to a personality which has become too one-sided."[14]

What part of *you* have you locked up, ignored, or resigned yourself to not enter except when absolutely necessary, if at all? This is your shadow. For purposes of the Five Elements, it's also your missing element. It's an entire room of yourself that you're not accessing or using. More importantly, it's the area of your life that holds the key to your transformation. It's time to open the door to your missing element and cultivate it to uplevel your life and work.

Embracing Your Missing Element

Most personality assessments are for the purpose of determining your personality type, similar to discovering your primary element in chapter 4. Knowing the category in which we fit makes us feel normal and unique all at the same time. It's why we love reading our horoscope or knowing our Enneagram numbers. We also get to compare with our friends to see how much we're alike, or different, and of course whether we're compatible. Reading about our personality assessment is usually a confirmation of what we already know about ourselves, but it can also act as a valuable mirroring technique. Sometimes it's hard to see ourselves, and so we need something to reflect back to us who we are and what we're good at. As interesting as this is, it can also limit our self-awareness by typecasting us into a category.

We tend to be relatively familiar with our strengths. In most cases, we repeat what we do best because we derive confidence and perhaps even a livelihood from it. For example, a professional tennis player probably hits over a million tennis balls over the course of her career. The more we do something, the more engrained it becomes in our brain. In fact, neuroscience shows us that approximately 95 percent of our behaviors are automatic, coming from our subconscious mind operating on autopilot.[15] Rarely do we do anything new or original. These patterns carve deep neural pathways in our brains. There's a reason we find ourselves "in a rut" when we continue doing the same thing over and over. As we gain praise, monetary gains, or notoriety for taking on certain skills and talents, we continue doing it more and more, digging these caverns even deeper. The same could be true when we cast ourselves as a certain type, such as "an attorney," "a Gemini," "a hot mess," "an academic," "a starving artist," or "the pretty one."

The ego loves to be defined, to be recognized, to be seen as someone specific and important. This shouldn't be denied. It's our way of making it through this world, socially and economically. However, there's more to us than a type, a name, or even a gender. We are multidimensional and living multiple lives and personas within one life. When we recognize and embody all our selves, we're able to uplevel our work and overall happiness.

By the time we reach adulthood, our patterns are well engrained. It takes present-moment consciousness, such as meditation, to create new neural pathways.[16] Scientific research in the field of neuroplasticity shows us that we can create new pathways and therefore patterns with repetition and reinforcement. We are not "hardwired" like we once thought. Or perhaps we were hardwired until our minds opened up enough to find out we're not. We can retrain our brain, or more specifically, we can create new roads or even an interstate system that is more efficient than the same dirt road we usually take. These new roads include your missing element with the interstate system being the Five Elements. By integrating your missing element, you won't be changing who you are, only expanding what you're capable of achieving.

After completing the Five Elements Quiz in chapter 4, you have your full profile that identifies your primary element and your missing element. Your missing element is the element in which you scored the lowest. You'll likely recognize it as the one you've denied, ignored, given up, or been challenged by throughout your life. You may have even formed an identity around this element as someone who you aren't. *I can never sit still in meditation. I'm not a runner. I'm just not organized. I'm not a public speaker.* There's a common adage that says, "Argue for your limitations and you'll win every time." If you declare what you're not, you'll always be right. Where you find you limit yourself through excuses or identities, you'll also find your missing element.

You may have had a tie for two of the elements. If this is the case, you can spot your true missing element by reading the descriptions for each element in chapter 5. You'll likely recognize that it's definitely *not* you. It's the one that jumps out as the most challenging to you. If not, think back to projects or creative pursuits or even personal relationships. At which stage in the process do you stop and walk away, or with which you become uncomfortably challenged?

If you scored relatively even on all the elements, you may be more of a jack-of-all-trades kind of person. And yet there is likely one of the elements that challenges you more than others or that you simply don't enjoy as much. Remember, we consist of *all* five energies and yet there's one that's your go-to and one that's your Achilles' heel.

My primary element is the Wood element. True to character, I love starting new projects. I usually wear multiple hats throughout my workday, managing multiple businesses I've created. When I have to invest all my energy into one project, I start to become bored, lose focus, and want to move on to something else. I probably have fifteen books on my computer that I've started writing. I have managed to complete books, including this one, but it's the Fire phase I slog through. I'd rather go from idea to editing (Metal being my second highest element) and skip the actual writing part. It's no coincidence that it's the Wood and Metal phases of projects in which I assist my clients.

Because I know I'm challenged by the Fire element phase, I intentionally integrate it into my life in small ways so that it doesn't become a deeper shadow. I use the example of a book as my creative project, but yours could be starting a new business, learning to play piano, an exercise program, a relationship, or even gardening. You may have heard the personal development phrase "How you do one thing is how you do everything." We can take incremental steps in any area of our life to create a positive ripple effect in all areas of our life. In other words, we can integrate our missing element in small ways to get big results. By consciously bringing your missing element into your daily life in easy ways, it will become more familiar and accessible. It will no longer be missing. In fact, you might find it opens a whole new world that you really enjoy.

In the case of my book coaching client, Stephanie, she had hundreds of pages that she had written on various healing topics that were a jumble of ideas without direction. After learning about the Five Elements Cycle, she realized she was missing the Metal phase. She needed organization of her materials—not just organizing it logistically in files, but organizing in terms of a theme, titles, and chapters. Once she started adding the Metal phase, she realized how much content she had that was publishable. It felt refreshing to see her work in a new light. She was adding practicality to the years of creative writing she'd done. This pivot allowed her to start seeing herself as a professional writer. In turn, she began entering her work into contests and for publication to online magazines.

As we open up to embrace our foreign element, we become more fluent in its language. It will no longer be a big albatross out to get you. Moreover, when you're faced with a situation that presents your missing element, you'll be able to handle it with compassion for yourself rather than fear. The first step with any change is having awareness of it. Now that you are aware of your missing element and recognize it as an underutilized part of you, let's look at practical ways to activate this element and bring it into your life, starting with your immediate environment.

How Your Workspace Affects Your Energy

If your parents were like mine, then you likely heard the phrase "you are who you hang out with." This implies that we are chameleons mirroring the people in our lives, or we are at least heavily influenced by them. As a feng shui expert, I would say the same holds true for our physical environment: you become what you surround yourself with.

The foundation of my work as a feng shui expert is that our home is a mirror of ourselves, and when you make changes to your space, you make changes to your life. In other words, feng shui is a tool used to make positive changes in our life. The fact that your home looks and feels better is just a by-product of these energy shifts. When feng shui changes are made and change happens soon thereafter, it can seem miraculous. However, it's simply the way energy works. Our home is an energetic extension of ourselves, so shifting energy in your home will cause a ripple effect of changes in your life.

We've all experienced an immediate shift in a room by simply painting it a different color. A pastel-colored room is going to have a different feeling than a room painted red. This may sound like common sense, not feng shui, but the principle is the same. Making changes to a space will illicit energy shifts in that space. More importantly, the energy shift affects the occupant of that space who in turn shift their energy in accordance. It's this shift that creates a domino of changes.

For example, adding a companion nightstand where there wasn't one before will shift the energy in the room to feel more balanced and supportive. This will be felt by the occupants and a change in their relationship will occur as a result. I've had clients whose relationship shifted immediately for the better. However, in some cases, the energy of balance wasn't something the couple's energy could support and resulted in their relationship ending soon thereafter.

Everyone is sensitive to the energy in a room, with the only variable being how conscious one is of those feelings. Highly sensitive people are more attuned to their emotional body and thus have a conscious appreciation for changes in their space. Even if not sensitive to energy, the subconscious mind and body will register the changes and elicit a corresponding reaction regardless of your conscious awareness.

These same principles apply to a workspace, inside or outside the home. I shudder when clients tell me they decorated their office with items they didn't want in their home. Many people don't give their office decor much thought despite the fact that it significantly affects their energy all day. Studies now show that one's workspace significantly influences productivity.[17] If you spend most of your time and energy in your workspace, then it needs to be a space that not only energetically supports you, but also boosts your productivity and overall morale. Of course, this is true for any space in which we spend a significant amount of time.

Most people see interiors as a one-time fixed application, but it doesn't have to be that way. It is changeable. Although you're not going to switch out your desk every week, you can add flowers to your office, change the art on the wall, or adjust how light comes into the room. Simple changes can make a big difference in how you feel in your office and your productivity as a result. If you don't like being in your workspace, you will, consciously or subconsciously, find reasons not to work there. You'll be challenged with distractions, be less productive, or feel unfulfilled with your work.

Most office workers were forced to work from home as a result of the pandemic. This created a whole host of new problems for creating a workspace at home. We generally have more control over the décor and arrangement of our workspace when we work from home, but we're also faced with other limitations in the case of cohabitating with roommates or family members. Unless you already had a designated office space prior to the pandemic, you likely had to carve out space from which to work in your home.

Because we spend most of our time during the week in our workspace, it's important to be conscious with how this space affects our energy. As you make changes to your workspace, you will notice changes in your inner world. More specifically, as you bring in aspects of your missing element into your workspace, you will begin to integrate that element more fully. Your primary element is most likely already reflected in your space. In the succeeding chapters, you will learn easy, practical ways to bring in the element you need to help balance your space and therefore yourself. But first, I want to set you up to win by helping you position your desk in the power position.

Placing Your Desk in the Power Position

Before adjusting the elements in your workspace, it's important to arrange your desk in the power position. This concept applies to all element types and is the most important change anyone can make in their workspace. In feng shui, this position is called the *command position* or *power position*. If your desk is already positioned in the power position, then good job! If not, then this one change will make a sizeable difference in your work productivity and overall mood. In the case of one client, her husband's home office was shoved up against the wall in a built-out attic space. He had been out of work for months with no luck on the job front. After repositioning his desk into the power position, he received three job offers within the next week.

Hopefully, you're now wondering where the power position is. The power position is where you can see the door to enter the room. This means you're not facing a wall or having your back to the door coming into the space. When we can see the door coming into the room, we are in our power. This is the same reason we prefer not sitting with our back to the door in a restaurant. Regardless of whether anyone comes into your office, the fight-or-flight brain wants to feel in control. Likewise, if you face a wall while working, you will be unhappy, face limitations, and want to quit your job. If possible, you'll also want a solid wall behind you. This provides support. If there's a window in the room, then you want to be able to see out the window, not have your back to it. In some rooms it is not architecturally feasible to meet all the criteria of the power position, but the main point is to see the doorway. The power position also applies to the placement of your bed.

If you face a wall while working, you will be dissatisfied with your work and face limitations. If you work from home, then you'll likely find somewhere else from which to work that is in the power position even if you weren't aware of it until now. If you're working from the kitchen table, for example, you've most likely found the power spot of the room without realizing it. The same happens naturally in coffeeshops and restaurants where customers seat themselves. I would encourage you to rearrange your desk into the power position or work from somewhere in your home that is in the power position while also having a designated office.

In traditional corporate America, you'll notice that executives in the C-suite face the door coming into the office when sitting at their desk, whereas middle management have L-shaped desks that face the door halfway, and staff employees sit in cubicles with their backs to passersby. This is exemplary of the power structures within traditional corporations. Consider these desk positions when selecting the desk placement in your home office. Do you want to be in the position of an executive, middle management, or staff employee?

Branding Your Workspace

Another consideration applicable to all elements is how the energy of your workspace reflects your branding. You may not have thought about your space as being a part of your brand, especially if no one ever walks foot into your home office. However, in the same way a picture says a thousand words, your space does too. If you own your own business, then you most likely selected the logo, colors, marketing materials, and social feeds to reflect your brand. Your office space should also reflect that brand, or at least the feel of your brand. Even if no one ever sees your office, the energy it emits will reflect your business. For example, if you're in the healing arts selling a calm, healing, and zen vibe, but your workspace screams clutter and chaos, then there's a discordant energy that's not attracting the clientele you want.

For those employed by a company, the energy of your space is also important but in a different way. While the company determines its brand, your space should reflect the image you want to portray to colleagues and higher-ups within the company. While you might not be influential in terms of the company's brand, you are responsible for your own branding with regard to your role within the company. Think about what you want your personal brand to be. Most likely, it was communicated through your résumé. Professional? Organized? Creative? Genius-level smart? Efficient? Team player? When I was employed as an attorney, I found that it was not to my advantage to appear calm and zen because it looked as if I weren't busy enough. Years later, when I started an energy healing practice, however, my relaxing space was appreciated by clients.

In the same way your home is a mirror of your life, your workspace is a mirror for your work and career. When I used feng shui for clients' offices, their workspace showed me the state of their business. For example, one client's office space was flooded with photos of her children. She wondered why sales had slowed and her overall morale had dropped. It was clear she wanted to spend more time with her kids.

In another example, a client was trying to run a major company from her kitchen table. She'd hit a plateau with the company. When she finally upleveled to a designated office space, her company skyrocketed to a new level. In another example, a client's office at a major corporation was peppered with old awards from the company that dated back decades. I encouraged her to update her office as to not appear outdated within a growing company. She didn't take my advice and was let go soon thereafter.

Does your space reflect you as a hobbyist, someone stuck in the past, a disorganized stress case, or someone who prioritizes guests over career?[18] Your space doesn't lie. It is your subconscious mind in plain view. When we have conscious awareness of our subconscious, this is when we can make positive, lasting changes. Here's my three-step process to brand your workspace to be a vibrational match to the success you want and deserve.

Step 1: The Vision. Think of three words you want your business or work to reflect. This may be a similar process you went through in selecting your brand. For example, a businessperson might want to be seen as *professional, organized*, and *approachable*. For someone in the healing arts, your words could be *calm, zen*, and *relaxing*. For a creative, their branding descriptors could be *cutting edge, avant-garde, and creative*. Identify your three words. Consider creating a mood board around those words in Pinterest or Canva.

Step 2: The Reality. Now take an objective look at your office space. You might think in terms of what a client or colleague would think upon entering your workspace. What would their impression be? What descriptors would you use for it in its current state? *Messy, amateur,* or *boring*? You might also notice whether your words correlate with how you currently feel about your work. Most likely they do. Let's now turn your current reality into your desired vision.

Step 3: The Transformation. What changes can you make to reflect the energy you desire? Start with what you can declutter from the space. Remove items that don't fit your vision. After you've decluttered, add items that reflect your branding descriptors.

In addition to making the adjustments discussed in this section, chapters 7 through 11 will provide ways to integrate the Five Elements into your workspace by adding your missing element or any other element you want to incorporate into your daily life.

Going Beyond Your Comfort Zone

In addition to revamping your workspace to better support you, let's consider what happens outside of work. Most of us enjoy doing things we're good at, and then we do them over and over. We might even invest a lot of time with schooling or additional training until we master a certain skill. Think about the number of free throws a professional basketball player has practiced over the span of their life. These activities we invest time and perhaps training in could range from a passionate hobby to our work in the world, or the two could merge at some point if a hobby turns into a career.

My wife is genius at word games. She loves to play Boggle on her phone and is currently ranked number four among all Boggle players in the world, according to the Boggle app. Impressive, right? She plays me for sport. I've significantly stepped up my game as a result. The point is she has a natural proclivity to word games and the more she plays them, the better she gets. Although I don't have the natural talent she does, I continue to improve and now come within a few hundred points of her. This example can be applied across the board. We can learn and improve in anything we put our mind to. I'll never rank in the top ten of Boggle champs, or even in the top 100, but I might give my wife a scare every now and then. To date, she has kept her day job and has not become a professional Boggler.

The activities you gravitate toward naturally have a direct relationship to your primary element. But what if you were to take part in activities that are not your go-to? Yes, I'm suggesting doing something you're not good at that's outside your comfort zone. It's easy to fall into routines that become dull. This causes us to feel burnt out, and before long, life doesn't have the pizazz it once did. Author James Hollis makes a case in *The Middle Passage* for going outside our usual comfort zone in order to integrate our shadows. He suggests that when we are apprehensive about trying hobbies and activities "other than that which got us this far," this "may impede our desire to give energy to the neglected parts of the psyche."[19]

Anytime I find myself feeling bored with life, I realize it's because I haven't tried anything new and have instead stayed in my safe comfort zone. I believe that bored people are boring people. The last thing I want to be is a boring person. To grow, we must challenge ourselves beyond that with which we're comfortable. You may have seen a popular meme depicting a circle of one's comfort zone and beyond it is "where the magic happens" or "everything I want." I want to help you get beyond the bubble and into the space where magic happens.

In helping clients navigate clutter challenges, I noticed a common theme among those middle-aged and older. They were holding on to items that reminded them of when life was fun and carefree. In holding on to the item, it was a way of attempting to hold on to those feelings. Instead of living in this still-life version of the past, what they really yearned for was a sense of adventure and spontaneity in the now. We can avoid looking to the past for our sense of adventure by trying new things now.

I encourage you to go beyond your comfort zone and try something new, particularly as it relates to your missing element. You might be surprised by what you discover. It could open you up to a new world of people and places you would not otherwise experience. It could be an activity you enjoyed when you were younger but stopped doing as you got older because it wasn't "practical." Or maybe it's something that you've always wanted to do or try, but it seemed out of reach until now.

We're drawn toward those things that will bring us fulfillment, even if it doesn't make sense or isn't practical. For example, I love music more than anything in the world, but I have no music talent. Or at least that's the story I've told myself most of my life. During the pandemic, I learned to play the piano. It would have been easier when I was ten years old, but it's forty years later, and I'm doing it. I feel like new neural pathways are being paved each time I learn a new chord. I also have a story that I'm not good at writing fiction. I've bought this story all my life, and yet it won't leave me alone.

What's something you have a story about, but that urge never seems to go away no matter how much you try to suppress it?

With the world at our fingertips through phone apps, YouTube tutorials, and a plethora of online courses, there's really no excuse not to learn something new. During the quarantine in 2020, many people had time to take on new hobbies. In addition to playing the piano and writing, I subscribed to MasterClass and loved learning about so many different topics. We don't always have the luxury of time to try new things, but it's a matter of prioritizing your day. A meditation, yoga practice, or piano lesson can take as little as ten minutes a day.

In *Atomic Habits*, author James Clear says the best way to incorporate a new habit is through repetition.[20] It's not about how long you do the activity but the frequency in which you do it. I decided I would try it out to help create a more disciplined writing practice. I carved out each Tuesday night from 7:00 to 9:00 to write fiction. It worked. Even if I didn't write for the entire two hours, I showed up each Tuesday night for several months until it became a habit.

I then decided to help institute this habit for other writers and started a writing group that now meets weekly. What started out as a challenging goal is now the highlight of my week. This is an example of turning your missing element into a hidden strength. Chapters 7 through 11 will provide you with suggested activities for each element so that you can begin to integrate your missing element, along with any of the other elements, into your everyday.

You Are What You Wear

Did you know that your wardrobe is a dead giveaway of your primary element? Talk about wearing your emotions on your sleeve. Even if you don't think of yourself as sporting a particular stylized wardrobe, we all dress like our primary element, or at least vacillate between our top elements. I can sometimes look at a person and identify their primary element simply based on their clothing choices. If we dress like our element, imagine what would happen if one day we dressed like our missing element. Better yet, imagine if you could intentionally dress in the energy of the element you needed for a particular occasion. Cue the red power tie.

Each article of clothing you put on, in addition to accessories, is an outward expression of your energy. You might notice that on days you're feeling more introverted, you wear darker colors, whereas days you're feeling more social, you'll wear more color, patterns, or accessories. Our clothing plays a significant role in how we feel. There's nothing worse than leaving the house for the day in an outfit you don't like. You feel "off" all day. Our clothing is an unconscious expression of how we're feeling, but you can also use it as a conscious expression of how you want to feel.

We dress differently depending on the circumstances—casual around town, business at the office, athletic at the gym, lounge-like at home. You can take this a step further and incorporate your missing element into your wardrobe. In other words, consider trying on influences from the other element types when you need them. For example, if you have a big interview and want to stand out, then bring in the Fire element. Need to be more organized? Dress like a Metal element. More grounding? Earth element. Feeling like your inner poet needs to come out? Wear black for more of the Water element. Need to tap into your inner go-getter? Wood element, please. In chapters 7 through 11, you'll learn to dress for success to accommodate any mood and for any occasion using the Five Elements.

Becoming Your Hidden Strength

By incorporating your missing element into your workspace interiors, your day-to-day activities, and your wardrobe, you'll start embodying new aspects of yourself that have been dormant all your life or that need reawakening from years prior. In doing so, you will be able to embody this new strength into everything you do, from projects to relationships. More importantly, you'll experience more fulfillment, success, and satisfaction in your work and everyday life.

The following chapters will provide practical ways to integrate your missing element into your conscious awareness. From there, your missing element won't be so missing after all. You might find that it adds that missing puzzle piece to your life, which now feels complete. That missing piece will become your hidden strength that opens your world in new ways. You might also be inspired to learn how to bring all the elements into your life on an as-needed basis. Let's start with the Water element to open up the creative channels and let inspiration flow.

CHAPTER 7
Flow Like Water

> When you once get an idea in which you
> believe with all your heart, work it out.
> —Henry Ford

I f you're needing to integrate more Water into your life, consider yourself lucky. Who wouldn't want more time to sleep, dream, or indulge in a spa treatment? Easier said than done, especially if you're a Fire element with a party to attend or a Wood element with a business meeting to run. If Water is your missing element, then life is asking you to slow down and tap into the subtle realms where imagination lingers and creative ideas flourish. You might like the idea of dipping into the Water element, but allowing yourself to do so is another feat altogether. Consider this your permission slip. What might otherwise seem indulgent is actually your best path forward. Because the Water element is slow and dreamy without much to show for your efforts, it can be difficult to justify. However, trust the wisdom of the Five Elements and allow yourself to relax and let go.

As the Five Elements Cycle is completed in the Water phase, all energy that was harnessed in the Fire phase and refined in the Metal phase is now released in the Water phase. This could mean the end of a project or the end of a particular stage of a project. It's the postpartum depression after giving birth. All the buildup of energy over nine months is finished. It's common for creatives to experience this when a major project has completed or released. The end of anything, whether deemed good or bad, is not easy. But we have to completely let go before we can start something new. And that's the point: there will be something new. The "new" also begins in the Water phase. Within all endings are new beginnings. Those with their primary element in Water are a funnel of constant ideas. If your missing element is Water, then the goal of this chapter is to acclimate you to better access the flow of the Water phase.

Our most brilliant ideas come to us during the Water phase. For Albert Einstein, it was the experience of being on water that helped him detach and have inner reflection. He wrote a letter to friends while on a cruise ship in Panama, saying, "A cruise in the sea, is an excellent opportunity for maximum calm and reflection on ideas from a different perspective."[21] Nikola Tesla, who created over 300 patents and was credited for the invention of the radio, describes the process of how ideas would come to him in his autobiography: "When an idea presents itself it is, as a rule, crude and imperfect. Birth, growth and development are phases normal and natural. It was different with my invention. In the very moment I became conscious of it. I saw it fully developed and perfected."[22] He wrote in *Scientific American,* "The idea came like a flash of lightning and in an instant the truth was revealed. ... The images I saw were wonderfully sharp and clear and had the solidity of metal and stone."[23]

The birth, growth, and development phases that Tesla refers to as "normal and natural" are in essence the Five Elements Cycle with the final form having the "solidity of metal and stone," the final Metal phase. The "flash of lightning" he refers to is the Water phase.

Child psychologists have recommended that kids be bored over the summer to allow space for creativity as a contrast to their otherwise busy schedules.[24] Boredom is crucial in developing an internal world which then allows for creativity. One fear of children being fed so much content through our phones, not to mention binge watching streaming content, is that it doesn't provide space for us to be creative ourselves. These same principles are true for adults too.

If we overexert ourselves, we may be forced into the Water phase as a result of getting sick. I think we'd all agree that it's better to take preventative measures when possible. However, in today's technology-driven world, being plugged in 24/7 has become our normal way of operating. That is, until COVID forced us to slow down. The whole world was thrown into the yin energy of the Water element. I heard so many people say that they were in dire need of an intervention of sorts because their job had become too stressful leading up to the pandemic. The ability to work from home and avoid traffic gave them the reprieve they needed. They described it as pushing the pause button on life for a while. Of course, the shutdown caused new stressors, economically and socially, for many and for those on the front lines.

If Water is your missing element, then staying busy is your everyday. Instead, consider the idea of taking *inspired* action. Try saying yes to only the things that truly light you up. In other words, keep your action-oriented personality, but add a dose of spiritual inspiration so that your actions are ripe with creative possibility and are soul-filling and possibly world-changing. We use our energy more efficiently when we act from a place of inspiration rather than obligation.

You might be thinking, *How do you ever get anything done if you're only taking action on things that inspire you?* Believe it or not, I get inspired to unload the dishwasher ... sometimes. I think unloading the dishwasher is one of the most boring, laborious chores of all household duties. But there are days when unloading the dishwasher feels better than not unloading it. The feeling of clean dishes in the cabinet and a clear dishwasher is, well, inspiring.

I use a mundane example of unloading the dishwasher to show you how the smallest actions can come from a place of inspiration. Apply this same idea to other activities: meeting up with a friend for dinner, attending someone's wedding, taking on extra duties at work, or writing a book on your expertise. The inspiration could be the extra money you'll gain or the sheer joy of the activity. The clearer you are about your inspiration for doing something, rather than doing it out of obligation, the clearer your energy will be in doing it.

Making changes on the mental level can be challenging if not supported by changes in your immediate environment. Have you ever come back after a trip, a retreat, or even a healing session vowing to make changes? As soon as you step inside your home, things go back to the way they've always been. Our home holds our mental and emotional patterns. It is an externalization of our inner energy. As much as we want to make changes in our life, it's nearly impossible without also making shifts in our space too. The changes you make need not be major. Sometimes the quality of energy you shift goes further than the quantity of energy. For example, I've seen clients finally let go and forgive a former relationship by getting rid of a single sweatshirt. Our items carry emotional weight that holds us down and blocks us from moving forward.

Clearing the Soil to Plant Seeds

In winter, the trees and land are barren of life. Everything has died and simultaneously preparing for new life. This is the Water phase. Something has ended and something has not yet started. Our own cycles follow the seasons, especially for those who live in a seasonal climate. In winter, the cold days and dark nights force us indoors. This is a literal metaphor for going inward. Despite the busyness of the winter holidays in the Northern Hemisphere, the Tao forces life to slow down. When we go inward, our inner voice is more available. It's no coincidence that toward the end of the winter season, in the month of February, most divorces are filed. There's been time to ruminate. The soil must be cleared for new life to grow.

Despite the calendar, we each go through our own seasons depending on life circumstances. The Water phase, whether it occurs in Winter or not for you personally, is a great time to declutter. It's a time to contemplate what's supporting us and what's depleting us. Our things are density that can hold us down or lift us up. We should take inventory periodically to make this determination. As we change, our things change, and vice versa. In my book *Clutter Intervention: How Your Stuff Is Keeping You Stuck*, I discuss our stuff in terms of the identity with which it represents. As our identity changes and evolves over the course of our life, our things must change too. When we hold on to any item that no longer serves us, it becomes an anchor tethering us to the past without the ability to move forward. This applies to relationships, social associations, and careers.

For items related to work and career, you'll want to consider decluttering your workspace. In chapter 6, I suggested that you look at your workspace objectively to see if it matched the image of your work or business. Now do this in terms of each item in your workspace. Take inventory of its contents. Clutter can come in the form of unused or outdated supplies, ill-fitting décor items, or even seemingly benign awards and accolades you received years ago. Are you holding on to folders and binders that you "need"? I encourage you to reconsider whether that's really true. Do you have the energy of past jobs, careers, or personas lurking in your workspace? If so, it's time to clear the soil.

The same goes for what I call *visual clutter*. Visual clutter is the stuff you do use and need to keep, but it doesn't need to be sitting out. Scientific studies have now proven that a cluttered space leads to a cluttered mind.[25] Even though how much stuff feels good in a space differs for each person, we also know when our space has become too cluttered. We simply don't feel good being in it. For spaces with visual clutter issues, what I've found to be the problem most of the time is that drawers, cabinets, or closets in the vicinity are too full for the stuff sitting out to go into. The real problem is the clutter in the storage areas. Tackle those and then you can file or store away more of the things you do need instead of the magazines you'll never read or the workshop binder from ten years ago that you know you'll never need.

Once you've decluttered your workspace, you'll feel so much better. It's only then that I recommend you add anything new to your space. Otherwise, you're planting seeds over weeds. When you're ready to water those seeds, the next section will give you suggestions of how to add the Water element to your workspace.

Adding Water to Your Workspace

The more we can bring the outdoors in to our living spaces, the better we feel. The Five Elements are the bridge between us and nature, and the more we can bring them intentionally into our interiors, the more we enjoy spending time in those spaces. The Water element is certainly no exception. It instantly calms the nervous system. I'm fortunate to live thirty minutes from the ocean. When I drive through the canyon to the ocean, my body instantly softens when it sees the blue ocean. It's as if my cells suddenly come into an active relaxation. That makes sense physiologically since our cells primarily consist of water.

Any body of water can have positive effects. You're probably aware of your preference—a lake, river, sea, or ocean. A friend of mine is a triple Aries, which means she has an Aries sun, Aries moon, and Aries rising. Five Elements translation: lots of Fire. When she was house shopping, she had the choice to live with an ocean view, but she opted for a lake view. The ocean had too much energy for her, whereas the lake had a calming effect on her fiery energy. I personally love the expansive feel of seeing the ocean, so long as I'm doing it from land and not a cruise ship.

What's amazing about the Five Elements is that even if a beach or lake house isn't feasible, you can bring the Water element, or any of the elements, into your living space through artwork. If you want more ocean in your life, then hang a picture that depicts the ocean. If a lake calms your energy, then hang a serene landscape with a lake. This is also a great way to feature vacation photos of places you've visited. However, be mindful of the state of the water in artwork. Avoid rough seas, sinking ships, or the feeling of being underwater as these energies will be replicated in your work.

Artwork is in effect subliminal messages on your wall. Your subconscious works with symbols and imagery even when your conscious mind is busy with the task at hand. Aside from the proper elements represented, it's important that artwork imagery has a positive association for you. If you're unsure of the symbolic meaning in art or photos, consult a dream dictionary for the interpretation to find out what your subconscious mind has been registering of which you're not consciously aware.

Water Element Symbols
Color: Black, dark colors, blue, clear

Shape: Curvy, wavey, paisley, scrolls

Interiors: Glass, mirrored, acrylic

Fountains
The Water element can be brought into a space in its literal form with a water fountain. Water is a natural purifier of the air and the sound of water can be very relaxing. It's no wonder why indoor and outdoor water fountains are so popular. In spaces that use traditional feng shui, you will see an outdoor water fountain near the front entrance of the building as the water is an auspicious energy that brings good fortune and harmonious energy into the space. A fountain is also considered ideal just inside the front door. For office spaces, it's best to place a fountain in the back left corner from the doorway coming into the room to activate the money sector of the room.

Accessories
The Water element can be brought into spaces symbolically through glass décor or furnishings: for example, a glass desk, acrylic chairs, or glass vases. The shape associated with the Water element is wavy or curvilinear. You can think of the rolling waves of the ocean. This is emulated in patterns with curves, such as paisley, scrolls, or the infinity symbol. Tables and sofas with

curvature shape add a dreamy, lounge-like energy to a space that captures the essence of the Water element.

The use of color is also influential to our inner elemental balance. In thinking about colors for your workspace, always go with what you love first. Never settle with a color you don't like. Color is personal to our energy field. If you decide to add the Water element through color, consider using a shade of blue. The color blue is associated with water in our collective conscious and thus can be used symbolically to represent the Water element.

In feng shui, the Water element is associated with the color black. You might not think of water as being the color black, but think of the way water looks at night, especially when you look out onto a body of water at night with the moon's reflection on the water. These are all aspects of the Water element—reflective surfaces, such as mirrors and shiny things, the yin moon, and the yin nighttime. It's no wonder why creatives are often night owls.

Using black or a dark color can create a dramatic look that can be quite effective if done in moderation—for example, as an accent wall. A cozy nook can turn moody quick with too much of the Water element. No need to get waterlogged. There was a trend in the 1980s to use black finishes for the entire bathroom, including a black toilet, black sink, and black tile. This drenched the room that already had plenty of the Water element to begin with in the form of plumbing fixtures. It's no wonder the fad didn't last long.

Desk

A home office is generally not a high priority for those with Water being their primary element. They may instead prefer working in bed, on the couch, or wherever the mood strikes them. However, carving out a home office may be helpful to create a much-needed boundary between work, play, and personal life. For those wanting more Water influences, however, give yourself permission to escape the office to get out of your head and to find your creative flow. To strike a balance, consider a glass desk that gives the creative influences of the Water element, but with a metal or wood structure that helps ground the energy productively.

Water Elements for Workspaces
- Indoor water fountains
- Glass desks
- Glass vases
- Glass bottles
- Glass-top tables
- Mirrors
- Glass frames

Hopefully, you're now inspired to make changes to your workspace. The more you enjoy being in your space, the more relaxed you'll feel. When in doubt, a simple way to bring the Water element into your workspace is with a glass vase of flowers. Not only does the glass vase of water bring in the Water element, but fresh flowers always add a wonderful energy to any space for all element types. Let's now look at ways to prime your pump of ideas when not sitting at your desk.

Water Element Activities

A few years ago, I had the luxury of living within walking distance to the beautiful Self-Realization Fellowship Lake Shrine in Pacific Palisades that was founded by Paramahansa Yogananda. This free meditation garden sits on a small lake a couple of blocks from the Pacific Ocean. I would walk down at least once a week to meditate. On my way home, I also had the benefit of stopping by Starbucks for an afternoon chai. I cherished those walks, knowing that my time at this location was a gift.

On my walk home one day, completely out of thin air, I heard "missing element, hidden strength" in my ear. I knew immediately it was in reference to the Five Elements and that this was a book title. I jotted it down in the Notes app on my phone. That was over five years ago and that seed that was planted in the Water phase has now come around to sprout. Ideas have no concept of time. It's best to write them down when they come because you never know when they may come back around to your timeline.

I share this story as the perfect example of being in the flow of the Water element. I had just finished meditating. I was walking lackadaisically and enjoying the nice day. In other words, I was immersed in Water element activities. Perhaps being near bodies of water was also helpful. All of these added up to me being available to Spirit's messages. We all receive messages in different ways and it's important to know when that time is for you and how to better cultivate it. When we are still, we can hear our inner voice. Getting past the ego voice to hear the inner voice is an ongoing challenge for most anyone with the exception of monks who live in the Himalayan mountains. To hear our inner voice, we must wade through all the other voices in our head. Perhaps that's the reason it's easy to put off doing mindfulness techniques. The following activities will help you access your inner Water element to bring more of this soul-filled creative energy into your life.

Sleep

Because we live in a highly yang society that is constantly pulling our energy in multiple directions, most of us need more of the Water element even if it's not our missing element. If you feel like your energy is being overextended, it's important to incorporate more yin energy into your everyday. Sleep is our natural way of balancing out the yang energy that our daily activities demand. Without adequate sleep to counterbalance our waking lives, an imbalance occurs and disease can set in sooner or later. Avoiding sleep is not sustainable. In Tracee Stanley's book *Radiant Rest: Yoga Nidra for Deep Relaxation and Awakened Clarity*, she introduces the ancient practice of yoga nidra, or the yoga of sleep, as a way to access a deeper level of rest.[26]

For those in need of more of the Water element, more sleep is advisable. This is usually the case for Wood or Fire elements who've maxed themselves out. Better sleep promotes better dreaming, which is also a Water element activity. Consider placing a dream journal near your bed. The more dedication you give to your dreams, the more they'll come around. You might not be given the download for the next masterpiece, but your dreams might give you insight into what your subconscious mind is up to. This could be helpful since we create most of our reality from our subconscious mind. Consult a dream dictionary to decipher the symbols. Also keep in mind that dreaming is not only for nighttime. Take some time to dream and scheme in your waking life. Everything starts with a dream, a desire, or vision.

Meditation

Meditation is another yin activity that can be used to counterbalance the overstimulation we encounter daily. Scientific studies have proven the benefits of how meditation helps relax our minds and therefore our bodies. The benefits of meditation are now so recognized that even medical doctors are prescribing it. It's one of the simplest activities we can do for our health. So why is it so hard to do?

In the same way that mirrors represent the Water element in our décor, so too is the Water element in our psyche. When we're still, our ego is mirrored back to us. To hear our mind chatter beyond what we already live with sounds miserable. That's why we have entertainment—Netflix, playlists, podcasts, YouTube, TikTok, and so on—going nonstop to drown out our incessant mind, the *monkey mind*, as it's called in Buddhist traditions. Of course, the best way to get past anything is to go through it. You guessed it: I'm recommending meditation as a way to face your mirror and move beyond the egoic mind to connect with your inner voice that's much quieter.

Think of the mind in layers. Just hovering above your head is your conscious mind—the one with all the thoughts all day. It's this layer that we have to sit with, and if you do it long enough, the ego will surrender. Just beyond that is another level where you could connect with the higher mind. Call it your higher self, your guides, the field, or God. This is where the golden ticket ideas reside. Sometimes they drop down in our dream state or in a moment of relaxation, for example, in the shower, taking a walk, zoning out in a car ride. My best ideas come to me in the shower. I should keep a journal in my bathroom. The water rains down ideas right into my head as I'm spaced out in this monotonous activity. A meditation doesn't have to be sitting cross-legged on a cushion. It can be any activity in which you transcend the ego mind.

Movement

Water is the element that has no form. Try holding water in your cupped hand. Good luck. It will spill everywhere. It goes where it wants with little desire to be controlled. In fact, a well-constructed container (Earth element) is the only way to control water. To access your Water element, this flowing movement is what you want to emulate. Immersing yourself in water is an obvious way to flow with the Water element. There is a rhythm to swimming, or at least for real swimmers. My version of swimming consists of an ergonomic float with a cupholder. That works too. If swimming isn't accessible, you might try a flotation therapy studio where you lie in your own private tub that completely supports you and allows your muscles to give in and let go. When I lived in the desert for a year, I found the need to refill my Water element in contrast to the yang, dry desert conditions. A flotation studio was perfect.

Other movement activities include certain types of yoga, such as yin yoga, restorative yoga, and light vinyasa yoga. These, of course, are slower than, for example, hot yoga, which will be recommended later on to tap into your Fire element. Movement that is slow, rhythmic, and almost meditative is a great way to let go of the noisy voice in your head. Qigong and tai chi are other movement practices that can be done in a meditative way to promote the flow of energy in the body. Also, the practice known as Continuum Movement explores the fluidity of our body as a way to move through blocks and embody ourselves more fully.

Journaling

To add more waves to your inner ocean, consider a "morning pages" practice, inspired by Julia Cameron's The Artist's Way.[27] In the morning, we are closest to having access to our subconscious mind. As in our dreams, we can use this time to dump the ego thoughts out like a trashcan on paper. On some days, you might be able to tap into something more profound, but that's not the goal. I started a morning pages practice right before the COVID-19 outbreak and found this practice to be incredibly helpful in navigating the rollercoaster of emotions that year. Each morning, I would write three pages with my coffee.

The instructions for the morning pages practice recommends using a legal pad or something of insignificance because the stream of consciousness that flows is not intended for keeping. I followed her instructions, but what began to happen was a ton of ideas and insights would come each morning. I switched to my Moleskine journal and began journaling the state of the world for historical purposes that would one day perhaps be of significance. I try to maintain my morning pages practice and feel a little lost on days I don't. If journaling doesn't float your boat, then try some of the other Water activities listed below.

Water Element Activities
- Swimming
- Floating
- Continuum Movement
- Restorative or yin yoga
- Meditation
- Breathwork
- Sleeping/napping
- Journaling
- Painting
- Channeling
- Vision boarding
- Daydreaming

Water Element Wardrobe

Now that you have some ways of accessing the Water element through activities, let's take a look at how to add the Water element to your wardrobe. Those dominant in the Water element are easy to spot by their style of clothing. Their clothes will have a flowy style rather than a tailored fit, with black being their color of choice. You'll notice that creatives often wear black. This is their inner Water element expressing itself from the inside out. On days you're feeling more introspective, you might find yourself drawn to wearing black. I've noticed that I tend to wear a black shirt on Mondays. I think it's my way of not wanting to jump into the work week quite yet. As the week goes on, my palette brightens up a bit as I get an extra pep in my step.

If you feel too watery, then leave the black clothes in your closet for a while and opt for some color. You can see the benefits of connecting with your creativity in the Water phase, but too much of a good thing is, well, too much. Once you've drenched yourself in ideas, it's time to put them to use in the Wood phase.

If your missing element is the Water element, then your goal is to give yourself more time and space for the intangibles of life without worrying about output. That means letting go of control, letting go of things, and letting go of anything that has blocked you from your connection with source energy. From here, you can align with your purpose and your passion. When you have that, you can plant the right seeds and grow anything from there in the Wood phase. Use the following worksheet to journal your reflections on the Water element and how to incorporate more (or less) Water into your everyday.

Water Element Worksheet

Water Element Profile Ranking: _____

(primary, missing, other...)

- ☐ I need *more* of the Water element.
- ☐ I need *less* of the Water element.
- ☐ I am balanced in the Water element.

Insights about the role of the Water Element in my life and work:

_____

_____

_____

_____

Water Elements to add to workspace:

_____

_____

_____

Water Element activities to incorporate:

_____

_____

_____

Water Elements to include in wardrobe:

_____

_____

_____

Water Elements to eliminate, if needed:

_____

_____

_____

CHAPTER 8

Strategize a Plan with Wood

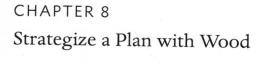

Do not fear going forward slowly; fear only to stand still.
—Chinese proverb

When I was kid, my parents would take my sister and me skiing out West each winter. The ski options within driving distance of Tennessee paled in comparison to the mountains in Colorado or the Sierras in California and Nevada. As soon as we could snap our boots into place, my sister and I would hop on the first available ski lift to take us up the mountain. We'd go from one trail to the next, catching whatever lift had the shortest line even if that meant skiing the back bowls or side trails. The only time we'd pull the trail map out was to find a bathroom or to meet up with my parents so that they could pay for lunch. My parents, on the other hand, would sit and study the trail map for about thirty minutes to plan their day of skiing before poling over to their first lift.

While I may talk a big game when it comes to snow skiing as a teenager, the truth is the older I get the more maps I need in life. There's more to lose. My parents had to be more careful and not end up on a black diamond slope. Not being as agile as us teenagers, they could have scooted their way down, while lift goers watched from above, or risked broken bones, resulting in a domino effect of losses. I prefer a map too when it comes to money and humility. But sticking too close to a map can also hinder the possibility of spontaneity or the chance to experience something even better than you could have planned. With or without a map, your inner Wood element got you to the ski slope and that's what counts.

Get Out the Map and Take the Lead

The Wood element is our inner leader, the pioneer or strategizer with the only variable being how closely we stick to the map. As you embrace your inner Wood element, you will feel more energetic, wide-eyed, and adventurous. If Wood is your missing element, then it's time to expand your world of possibilities. In 2013, I finally got the courage to follow my dream of living in California. I had no intent to make the drive alone or even by car, but I woke up on Independence Day and knew it was what I should do. Within a few months, I packed what was left of my belongings into my Prius, took off across I-40, and landed in Los Angeles four days later.

I had a map for getting there, but not for when I arrived. Being self-employed and single, I had nothing to ground me in the sprawling City of Angels, except for chasing dreams and unavailable relationships. Aside from a temporary rental and some rollerblades, I didn't have a plan. I was lost. I was meeting a lot of people and making a lot of contacts, but nothing stuck. I found myself driving from one side of the city to the other with nothing to ground me.

With more friends and clients still in Nashville, I traveled back and forth quite a bit. I ended up spending more quality time with my parents after I moved away than when I lived close by. Having that time with them ended up being a blessing since they passed away within five years of me moving away. I'm still integrating my own Earth element that I had relied on from my Earth element parents. After all, the Wood element can only continue growing if it has the proper foundation (Earth element) in which to do so. You can see how these elements rely on one another and when they're gone, we're forced to either find someone new to fill in the missing pieces, do it ourselves, or a combination of both.

If your missing element is Wood, then you might find yourself being attracted to people with big dreams who take action on them. Who we are attracted to, romantically or platonically, is a reflection of our own missing element that hasn't found expression yet. And what we see in others, we have within ourselves. In the following sections, you'll discover ways to cultivate more of the Wood element into your life, starting with your workspace.

Adding Wood to Your Workspace

If you need more Wood element in your life, the good news is that it's easy to come by in our living spaces. There are so many ways to bring wood into our space since wood makes up a lot of our interior finishes and furniture. As the flagship Wood element, trees are an invaluable source in architecture and interiors because of its strength and malleability. Let's look at some easy ways to bring the Wood element into your workspace.

Wood Element Symbols

Color: Shades of green

Shape: Columnar, tall, linear

Interiors: Wood surfaces, wood furniture

Desk

A wood desk or table is one of the best ways to bring wood into your workspace. A glass desk would also support the energy of the Wood element because glass being a Water element supports the Wood element. A desk made of metal would be ill-advised for those with a missing Wood element because metal cuts wood, thereby further diminishing the Wood element in the room. On the other hand, for those who tend to be overbalanced in Wood, a Metal desk or a desk that features metal hardware would be recommended.

Plants

Incorporating plants is one of the easiest ways to add the Wood element to your workspace. You can never go wrong with plants in your space (except for spikey plants that point toward you). Plants add the energy of growth, expansion, and life to a space—all essential qualities of the Wood element. Any by-product from trees and plants, such as cotton and linen, would also be considered a Wood element.

Plants aren't only touted by feng shui practitioners. Psychologists have found that plants in a workspace can improve employee productivity by 15 percent.[28] In feng shui, fake plants provide the same function as the Wood element. However, if you're averse to fake plants, then avoid using them. After all, it's your positive energy that's most important.

Accessories

Like plants and trees, the color *green* is associated with the Wood element in feng shui. Incorporating any shade of green can add the energetic qualities of Wood into your space. Although colors can be personal to us in our preferences, they also have significance in our collective consciousness. Green is associated with growth, money, health, and expansion—all the same energetic components of the Wood element.

The shape associated with the Wood element is columnar or anything vertical. Think of a tree and the way it draws your eye up as opposed to down. The number one is also an expression of the Wood element. The shape of the number one is columnar and represents independence and leadership, all qualities of the Wood element energy.

Wood Elements for Workspaces
- Plants and flowers
- Wood furniture, including chairs, tables, consoles, etc.
- Wood flooring
- Artwork with nature scenes
- Floor lamps
- Columns
- Vertical blinds
- Cotton (derivative of wood)
- Rugs
- Pillows, drapery, and fabrics

Wood Element Activities

Activities associated with the Wood element pick up where the Water activities left off. For example, if you journaled in the Water phase, you're actively writing in a more purposeful way in the Wood phase. If you enjoyed floating on a lazy river in the Water phase, you're now whitewater rafting in the Wood phase. There's an overlap in activities, but the Wood element prefers doing them a little faster and more purposefully. We'll see this same rise in intensity when we move from the Wood phase to the Fire phase.

Yoga

One of the reasons I love yoga is the many styles of yoga available depending on what your body needs. In the Water phase, restorative yoga is best. To stoke the Fire phase, it's power or hot yoga. To engage the Wood element, try vinyasa or hatha yoga. Like a bamboo tree, hatha yoga blends strength and flexibility. Stretching the muscles relates to the Water phase, whereas strengthening relates to the Fire phase. In the Wood phase, it's important to both strengthen and stretch our muscles proportionately for a yin-yang balance.

Walking

If the Wood element is your missing element, then chances are the Wood element activities may not be activities you regularly engage in on a regular basis. One of the easiest ways to start is by taking walks. Try taking a walk at least three times a week, if not daily. The CDC recommends adults get at least two hours of aerobic physical activity, such as a fast-paced walk, per week for at least ten minutes at a time to maintain a healthy weight and prevent disease.[29]

In certain areas around the world, known as Blue Zones, there is a high rate of centenarians who live well into their hundreds with little or no disease. Their lifestyle has been studied to figure out their secret to longevity. In addition to certain diets, walking is a regular part of their lifestyle and their primary mode of transportation. The Blue Zone inhabitants walk at least an hour a day, with an emphasis on not overworking the body. They suggest to ride a bike or swim every other day for thirty to forty minutes, including on weekends.[30] Not only will Wood activities help activate the Wood element, but they will also help you stay healthy.

Forward-Movement Activities

If Wood is your missing element, I challenge you to do a Wood activity that you're not used to doing. The Wood element activities are action-oriented but not as hard-core as the Fire element activities. Think a morning walk with your dog rather than CrossFit training. Any activity that involves forward movement engages your inner Wood element. For someone who initially had no desire to drive long distances, I was surprised by how much I enjoyed driving cross-country from Tennessee to California. For four days, all I did was move forward at a steady pace (sometimes a little too fast). The overall journey felt like I was moving forward on my life path with the drive being a literal metaphor. Since then, I enjoy driving, especially day trips up the coast. You might be surprised at how you can turn a Wood activity into your favorite activity. You might find that it helps you stroll along your life path too.

Wood Element Activities

- Walking
- Hiking
- Skiing
- Active water sports
- Bicycling
- Vinyasa or hatha yoga
- Weight training
- Writing
- Driving

Wood Element Wardrobe

As with all the elements, the Wood element dresses in accordance with its quintessential properties. For Wood elements, that means clothing that allows one to be flexible and adaptable to any occasion—a business meeting, walking to lunch, or a yoga class after work. Because a Wood element is on the move, versatile, and practical, natural fabrics like cotton or linen is their go-to fabric with a bent toward greens, denim, and natural colors. It's no coincidence that cotton is literally made from Wood. Shoes are comfortable, practical, but stylish. Joggers and T-shirts are the usual attire on the weekends.

Those native in the Wood element are generally slender and wear clothing with ease—not baggy nor overly tight. They may have invented smart casual in order to pivot in any direction needed at a moment's notice by throwing on a blazer for an important meeting and then rolling up their sleeves for working solo on the computer or taking a walk during lunch. On days you need to embrace your inner Wood, consider wearing clothing that's versatile and practical that can assist you in taking action and getting things marked off your to-do list, including that afternoon walk or yoga class. While Wood elements may not turn heads with fashion, they will impress with their productivity. When it's time to take the spotlight, you can toss the sensible shoes for high heels and ignite your inner Fire element.

Wood Element Worksheet

Wood Element Profile Ranking: _____

(primary, missing, other...)

- ❑ I need *more* of the Wood element.
- ❑ I need *less* of the Wood element.
- ❑ I am balanced in the Wood element.

Insights about the role of the Wood Element in my life and work:

_____

_____

_____

_____

Wood Elements to add to workspace:

_____

_____

_____

Wood Element activities to incorporate:

_____

_____

_____

Wood Elements to include in wardrobe:

_____

_____

_____

Wood Elements to eliminate, if needed:

_____

_____

_____

CHAPTER 9
Light Your Fire

What matters most is how well you walk through the fire.
—Charles Bukowski

As I walked from the green room toward the ABC studio stage, I gave a head nod to Ralph Fiennes who had just finished his segment. I was a huge fan of his films *The Reader* and *The Constant Gardener* and was awestruck by the fact that we were slated for the same episode. My segment was the last of that day's episode which gave me plenty of time to be nervous. Because they stick the decluttering non-celebrity at the end of the show, I'd had fifty-seven minutes to build up nerves. As I walked toward the stage, I thought I might pass out. When they call the show *Live with Kelly and Ryan*, that means it's literally *live* before a studio audience and national TV. No editing.

Just breathe, I kept telling myself, *just breathe*. As I made my way from behind the curtain to the floor, I could feel the lights and hear the audience. And then a calm came over me. And away I went with the segment. Within two minutes and twelve seconds, it was over. I did it. And by *did it*, I mean I didn't trip or stumble over my words. In other words, I hadn't embarrassed myself on national television.

Kelly Ripa was incredibly gracious and seasoned at keeping rookies like me calm. Ryan Seacrest had flown the red-eye from California to New York to get to the show in the nick of time from hosting *American Idol* the night before. I had taken the same flight just twenty-four hours before and recognized the red-eyed coffee buzz. Between the flight, the time zone change, nerves, and it being a morning show, I was about twenty hours behind on sleep myself. Ryan's lack of sleep turned into distracting antics for which I was grateful. Friends later asked how I was able to focus with him running all over the stage. It's because he is a Fire element and I'm a Wood element. I prefer to pair with a Fire element who can be the more expressive one. And the Fire element loves to pair with someone who allows them to take the spotlight. I'm the kindling that helps light the fire. And yet I still had to work with my inner Fire element to get the courage to say yes and show up on that stage.

Even though we can never be all elements, there are times when we need to access all five of the elements. Fire is the element that I continually work to integrate in order to accomplish the work I want to do in the world. Like most authors, I'm more comfortable being an introverted writer. But being an author also includes promoting your book and thus taking on aspects of the Fire element at times. Like most people's missing element, it's the element that I'm most uncomfortable with and yet most drawn to.

The Fire element is the most yang of all the elements. In other words, it is the highest expression of energy. For this reason, Fire element folks are alluring, magnetic, full of enthusiasm, and charismatic. Although not an exact comparison, Fire elements are most akin to the fire element signs in Western astrology: Leo, Sagittarius, and Aries. If you have one of these as your sun, moon, or rising sign, then aspects of the Fire element are familiar to you.

Let Your Light Shine

If Fire is your missing element or one of the lower elements in your profile, you might be intimidated by the prospect of taking on the Fire element qualities. It feels risky and scary to be so out, loud, and proud. This may be true even if your primary element is in Fire. We all experience fear about situations, but the difference is moving through it despite the fear. The Fire energy burns through the fear with enthusiasm, passion, or love.

Anyone can embody the Fire element with practice. Whatever we put our attention on expands. You may have heard the phrase "Where attention goes, energy flows." This goes for all the elements. Set an intention for what you want more of, put your attention on whatever it is, and opportunities will show up to help you. Fire elements are powerful manifesters when they're able to focus their energy on something specific. Think of a laser beam piercing through an object. This is the intensity of energy that Fire elements possess and you can too if you so desire.

Even if the Fire element isn't your missing element, there may be times in your life when you feel like you're running on reserves. Perhaps you lack the usual passion or gusto for life. Without enough of the Fire element, you can feel tired, unfocused, unproductive, lethargic, and an overall feeling of purposelessness. I know when I'm not in the mood to do yoga or some other form of exercise, that's when I need it the most. Unless you're burnt out from doing too much, it's likely you need to relight your fire. If you need help in lighting your inner Fire element, then you can always look to the Wood element for help.

Like putting a log on the fire or using kindling to start a fire, the Wood element helps keep the energy moving. Instead of going for a run, maybe a walk is what you need, and it could possibly lead to a fast walk as you get your momentum. This example can be taken literally or metaphorically as a way to access your inner Fire element.

As you start to embrace your inner Fire element, you'll inevitably rub up against fear because your Fire is your inner light. It's the highest expression of *you*. It's the pinnacle energy of being seen in the world, and that's scary, especially for the introverted Metal element, the inward Water element, or the comfort-seeking Earth element. However, by integrating the Fire element in small doses and on an as-needed basis, you'll be able to better acclimate to the heat.

Adding Fire to Your Workspace

On days when I need extra energy before sitting down to write, I light a candle or burn incense. I call in the Fire element to assist me. Fire is one of the most amazing expressions of nature. It's also one of the most destructive forces on the planet in the form of volcanic molten spewing from earth or forest fires that ravage the land. Without fire, however, there would be no life on Earth. The source of all our energy is the sun—the grandest of all Fire elements in our galaxy. It's the energy from the sun that provides the elemental conditions that allows for all fire and light. It's how we can magically flick a lighter with our thumb and, voilà, a candle illuminates a room. On cold or cloudy days, the extra energy from a candle, along with a warm cup of tea, is exactly what I need to jump-start my morning. It's these small touches that can make big shifts in our energy.

As with any of the elements, the Fire element can be used in spaces in its raw, natural form or in symbolic colors and shapes. The Fire element can also be used symbolically as the color red or anything triangular-shaped, in addition to artificial lights or LED candles that mimic a flame. Some examples are provided in the following sections.

Fire Element Symbols

Color: Red, bright orange, sunshine yellow

Shape: Triangle or cone-shaped

Interiors: Fireplace, stove, lights

Lighting

Since the sun is the ultimate Fire element, allowing more natural light into your space will immediately increase the yang qualities in a room. We can manipulate the natural light that comes into the space as well as use artificial lighting. Studies have shown that natural light in offices improves sleep, increases exercise, and supports overall well-being.[31] In a study conducted by advisory firm Future Workplace, researchers found that "access to natural light and views of the outdoors" was the most valued attribute of the workplace environment, ranking above perks such as on-site cafeterias, fitness centers, and childcare.[32] We are naturally drawn to natural light and the outdoors, even if only a view of the outside.

Whether you work from home or outside the home, the amount of natural light in your workspace has likely been a consideration. Now you know why. It's the Fire element and it literally gives you energy. Adjusting the lighting in your workspace can have the most dramatic change in how you use and enjoy your space. Adjust natural light with blinds or curtains as if it's a dimmer switch, anywhere from all the way bright to all the way dark. Windows will take on the opposite effect at night by sucking energy from a room rather than giving energy to a room, so adjust the window covering each morning and each night.

You can make further adjustments to the room with artificial lighting and lamps, which is especially needed in the winter months and, of course, at night. I recommend varying up the light sources in a room with a combination of uplighting and downlighting. If you only use the overhead light, the room will look dull and one-dimensional. If you must use the overhead light, pair it with a floor lamp or table lamp that casts the light out into the room or up toward the ceiling. Also consider using a task light that emits directly onto your workspace. This will help you focus on the task at hand as if someone were holding a spotlight over your work.

Candles

Candles have become a popular décor and gift item for homes. High-end candlemakers now use ingredients that rival the best perfumeries. In addition to the décor and olfactory senses they promote, candles are also a great way to incorporate the Fire element fire into your space. If actual fire is unsafe or disallowed, as is the case with some commercial spaces, consider using LED candles that have a flickering effect that tricks the brain into thinking it's real. You can also use a candle as part of an intentional ritual for your workday. As you light it, call in your guides, helpers, or your muse, along with an intention for this time. You can also use the candle as a meditation anchor. Gaze into the flame as a point of focus. This is a form of meditation that will recharge you.

Desk

You would think a red desk would be hard to find, but not for Fire element people. I've been astounded by how many of my clients who are dominant in the Fire element have a red desk. Like attracts like, but is that always a good thing? It so happened that these clients also needed help with better focus. Too much fire leads to scattered and unfocused thinking, and so I wouldn't recommend a red desk for those who have their primary element in Fire. If Fire is your missing element, then a red desk would be great, but you're likely to not want one. That's okay; a red desk isn't for everyone. The Wood element supports the Fire element, and thus, a wood desk would be a good choice. Avoid a glass desk if you're trying to boost your Fire element because water puts out fire. For those with their primary element in Fire, however, a glass desk would be calming and creative.

Accessories

You can add the Fire element to your workspace by adding a splash of red, yellow, or orange to your accessories. While you don't want to go overboard, adding a touch of these bright colors to your workspace in the form of artwork, books, candles, and picture frames will add a spark of energy. My favorite color is yellow and I keep my sunshine-yellow water bottle on my desk to brighten up my workspace. Items made from or inspired by animals are also considered Fire elements. While I'm not a proponent of killing animals for the sake of our interiors, artificial patterns of animal skins, vegan cowhide, or a furry blanket can add a fire quality to a space.

Accessories in the shape of a triangle can also create the energetic qualities of the Fire element. The triangle or cone-shape is not a common shape in interiors, but if you have something pyramid-shaped, you can use it intentionally to add Fire to your space. You'll often find gemstones shaped as pyramids for the purpose of focusing the energy of that stone's metaphysical properties. Also orienting furniture at a diagonal can create this dynamic Fire quality, as does arranging items in threes. The number three represents creative energy and thus adds energy to the room and therefore its occupants. As a side note, I don't recommend making these Fire adjustments in the bedroom as it can create triangulation in your relationship.

Fire Elements for Workspaces
- Candles
- Lighting
- Triangular lampshades
- Pyramid shapes
- Pets
- Leather upholstery
- Wool upholstery
- Animal skin rugs or throws
- Artwork depicting any of the above

Fire Element Activities

As the most action-oriented of all the elements, Fire elements love to move, exercise, sweat, and socialize. If you need more of the Fire element in your life, then I recommend more movement in your daily life. This is your nudge to exercise more. When you exert energy, your body naturally creates more energy to replenish it. You've most likely had the experience of forcing yourself to the gym or an exercise class despite being completely exhausted. By the end, you feel so much better and probably more energetic than you did going into the gym. That's the case with Fire-related activities. Because the Fire element is the highest expression of our energy, it can activate an adrenaline response. Some runners or high-impact athletes refer to themselves as adrenaline junkies who need more and more adrenaline to feed their brain. This could be an indication of an overbalance of Fire. For those needing more of the Fire element, however, I suggest some of the activities listed next.

High-Impact Activities

You'll notice that some of the suggested Fire activities are similar to the Wood activities in the previous chapter because both elements are action-oriented and love movement. However, a true Fire element will prefer activities with more intensity: for example, running instead of walking. While I encourage you to go outside your comfort zone, you should also always listen to your body. Fire activities are not for everyone. If I were to go for a run this afternoon, I'd most likely pull a muscle and be on my back for a week. I've learned to not get roped into going to a CrossFit class when a friend tries to talk me into it. My body has never been made for high impact sports even when I was super fit in my twenties. Different body types are made for different physical activities. As a former yoga instructor, I was taught to instruct students to find their edge, meaning go as far as you can without going too far to cause an injury. As you try the Fire element activities, I suggest finding your edge.

Speaking, Social Media, and Socializing

If the subheading for this section scares the hell out of you, then you're not alone. These S-words are the bane of existence for most Water, Metal, and some Earth elements. Maybe the CrossFit class doesn't sound so bad after all. Those native to the Fire element are outgoing and enjoy interacting with other. Socializing in-person and online is an important aspect of networking for those who are in the position of generating sales and clients. Fire elements feel right at home with social activities and may even derive their income from such activities. However, if you have a missing Fire element, you're unlikely to enjoy the level of socializing as a true Fire element does.

The *I Ching* translation for the Fire element is "the clinging." It's through gathering energy within oneself and with others that we bring the energy of a project or an event to its highest potential. Whenever I have an idea for a social gathering, like a pool party or birthday get-together, I know it's best to turn the idea over to my wife, who is primarily a Fire element. She gathers enthusiasm around the idea, which has a way of gaining momentum. I take care of the necessary details from there. With her enthusiasm, we end up with a high turnout rate at any gathering we have, much more than if had it been me who tried to execute the Fire phase.

It's possible that you could find some of these Fire activities rewarding or enriching to your life if approached intentionally and with compassion for yourself. A friend of mine, who is a primary Water element, would develop hives every time she spoke in public. Because she had a desire and need to do more public speaking for her business, she decided to join Toastmasters, an international club to help build speaking skills. Although she's not an international keynote speaker as a result, she was able to break through her fears and can now hold speaking engagements without hives. More importantly, she now enjoys speaking at events and engaging with the audience.

Fire Element Activities

- Running
- Hiking
- Spinning or cycling
- Hot yoga
- Socializing
- CrossFit
- Acting or improv classes
- Public speaking
- Screenwriting
- Social media
- Horseback riding

Fire Element Wardrobe

It's easy to spot a Fire element in a crowd. They like to be seen and their outfit is no exception. People with a primary Fire element wear bold colors, dress fashionably, and love to accessorize. When dressed down, they may be sporting the latest fitness wear. For men, their attire may include activewear, graphic T-shirts, bold colors, and of course the power red tie.

If you're needing more Fire, bold colors and accessories may not be your thing. That's okay—you don't have to be someone you're not. There's nothing worse than wearing clothes that you don't like. However, there may be occasions when you might want to make a bolder impression. There's a reason for the power red tie. According to a HuffPost article, a red tie communicates power, passion, and victory. A blue tie says you're calm and hardworking, while a yellow tie expresses your creativity and exuberance.[33] The same translation of colors would apply to any clothing items for men and women. The same could be true for attending a social event at which you'd like to stand out in order to meet someone new or for power networking. Add a splash of color or a few extra jewelry accessories than usual. As your wardrobe glitters, you might find that you also start to shine a bit more on the inside and out.

Fire Element Worksheet

Fire Element Profile Ranking: _____

(primary, missing, other…)

- ❑ I need *more* of the Fire element.
- ❑ I need *less* of the Fire element.
- ❑ I am balanced in the Fire element.

Insights about the role of the Fire Element in my life and work:

_____

_____

_____

_____

Fire elements to add to workspace:

_____

_____

_____

Fire element activities to incorporate:

_____

_____

_____

Fire elements to include in wardrobe:

_____

_____

_____

Fire Elements to eliminate, if needed:

_____

_____

_____

CHAPTER 10
Ground into Earth

Listen, are you breathing just a little, and calling it a life?
—Mary Oliver

I magine if there were no pause between the inhale and exhale breath. This is what happens when we rush from one thing to the next without time to properly transition, whether it be errands or a major life change. This is a way of life for those with a missing Earth element. We all need time and space to pause, transition, and breathe. And all creative endeavors need time to rest after enduring the Fire phase in order to review, reassess, and strategize for success. The Earth element gives us the space to do just that in all areas of our life.

If you're missing the Earth element or scored low on it, then you're needing to spend more time setting a strong foundation for projects and relationships. This simply translates to taking more time with the task at hand. This is essential to the financial success of any busines or project you take on. At the beginning of *Oprah's Super Soul* podcast, Oprah Winfrey starts each show with an introduction, saying, "I believe one of the most valuable gifts you can give yourself is … time … taking time to be more fully present."[34] This is the essence of the Earth element. The Earth element phase is unassuming in its importance, as are Earth element people in general.

Taking Time to Invest in You

The Earth element is the secret to success that no one tells you (except Oprah). In fact, Earth signs in Western astrology, which include Taurus, Capricorn, and Virgo, are known for their money-making abilities. Money is an earthly concept. This is the reason why some spiritual-minded people struggle financially. They are not grounded to earth to be part of the exchange of this earth-bound transaction.

When in balance, the Earth element is a bounty of abundance. It's the harvest of crops after the growth season of summer. The Earth element is in essence a container. Think of money bags, a pocket full of cash, or a pot of gold. It's also the holder for anything we want to contain. For example, an earthen basin holds water, a house holds its people and things, a purse holds money, and an Earth element person holds space for others. For those who don't come by the Earth element naturally, how can you do this for yourself? How can you hold more space for yourself and become a container for all that you desire on this Earth?

If you're realizing that you need more of the Earth element in your life, then you likely scored high in the Water, Wood, or Fire element. The primary Water element often avoids the confinement of the Earth element. It wants to flow with all her ideas and no real commitment. For people dominant in the Wood element, you are inclined to skip steps in your current project or lunge forward into your next venture. In doing so, you fail to build a proper foundation. What you set out to accomplish either never gets off the ground, or you have to go back and lay proper groundwork. It's like trying to build a house by putting walls up before the foundation has been poured. This is a common challenge for Wood and Fire elements. Self-care, which is an aspect of the Earth element, gets overlooked, and before you know it, you're plunged back into the Water element, rather taking time out in the Earth element.

The Earth element has been one of my missing elements since I moved from my hometown of Nashville to Los Angeles. Nashville is a super grounded city that epitomizes the Earth element, as it sits in a bowl-shaped terrain with a focus on home and family. People who intend to move there temporarily end up staying much longer. It's hard to move from Earth energy. It holds you in place and makes it challenging to move. Compare that to the sprawling City of Angels that sits on a fault line where people go to chase their dreams. For a big city, a lot of emphasis is placed on spaces in Los Angeles. Having a home in which you feel grounded is the key to staying put in this otherwise transitional city. Your space is your only anchor. It's no wonder Angelenos escape the city for the Earth desertscape when needing to recharge.

I'm finally learning to integrate the Earth element more fully and appreciating the gifts it has to offer. I've found this to be true in my work. Instead of rushing to push a new product, book, or business out, I've learned to take my time to not skip over the necessary foundational structures. This has also been the case for romantic relationships. With the excitement of new love, my tendency had been to skip over the getting-to-know-you parts and jump into the deep end of living together and marriage. My soul finally forced me to get it right with my current marriage because we were friends for almost ten years prior to dating.

If you are low in the Earth element, then you may notice yourself being anxious, unable to relax, unfocused, brain foggy, or spaced-out. Acupuncture can help build your Earth element (or any of the elements), as these issues will always be mirrored in our physical health over time. Before it hits you on the level of the physical body, let's look at ways of incorporating the Earth element into your everyday so that you can have a built-in foundation for yourself.

Adding Earth to Your Workspace

Do you have a friend whose home you love going to? Before you know it, you're sunk down into a cozy couch with a tea and a blanket not wanting to leave. Or maybe you find that people do that in your home. These are the hallmarks of an Earth element's home. The interior of the Earth element's home is cozy, warm, and grounding. If you've realized you need more of the Earth element in your life, then these are the themes to integrate into your space.

The Earth element is best exemplified by the Southwest United States or other desert areas around the world. Most homes in Arizona, New Mexico, and parts of California are made of adobe, which is clay made from the dirt native to those regions. This is the Earth element. Remember playing in the dirt as a kid? It was natural to get dirty. Some adults still get their hands dirty, but in more structured ways by planting flowers and landscaping. These are examples of engaging with the Earth element and feeling grounded with Mother Earth.

Like all the elements, the Earth element can be used in your interiors in a variety of symbolic ways to encapsulate its energy. If your space feels cold or sterile, then you'll especially want to consider adding some of the suggested Earth elements. Modern or contemporary styles of decorating, which are heavy in the

Metal and Water elements, oftentimes need warming up with the Earth element. A few touches of the Earth element will go a long way to making your space more comfortable and inviting for you and other occupants. With too many Earth elements in your space, you might have a hard time getting people to leave your home or workspace. If it is enveloped in too much of the Earth element, it can be challenging to find movement again. This can be a challenge for those with a primary Earth element.

Interior designers of commercial spaces must take these considerations into account when selecting furniture. For example, is it a space that encourages people to stay a long time versus a space where they want a quick turnover of people? The changing interiors at Starbucks chains are a great example. At one point, they had cushy armchairs. This resulted in people staying for hours, using the internet, and only buying a cup of coffee. At many locations, they switched to stand-up tables to encourage people to not stay so long. Now their stores are a combination of seating depending on the community and vibe for each location. Think about this in terms of your own space. Consider whether you need more or less of the Earth element depending on whether you need more or less movement in your workspace. Do you need more comfortable interiors for yourself or clients in order to have more quality time, or do you need a space with more action at a quicker pace? Adjust seating and table surfaces accordingly.

Earth Element Symbols

Color: Earth tones of yellow, orange, maroon, and brown

Shape: Square or rectangle

Interiors: Clay, terra cotta, tile, containers

Clay Pots and Containers

With dirt being the essence of the Earth element, anything made from dirt is considered an Earth element. Therefore, the use of clay in the form of pottery, tile, or terra cotta is a great way to bring the Earth element into your space. It's interesting to note that the process by which clay hardens to become a solid substance is by the application of the Fire element. Fire creates Earth in the Five Elements Cycle. In the same way the molten lava spewed from volcanoes creates new earth, so does fire in the process of creating pottery. These two elements pair well together in a space. In fact, you'll often see the Fire and Earth symbols together in Southwestern motifs with a combination of squares and triangles. Earth tones, such as orange, yellow, and brown, are Earth elements and often used in combination with red, the Fire element.

In addition to clay pots being used as an Earth element, any container, such as a basket or a box, is considered an Earth element. This makes Earth elements particularly handy when it comes to workspaces. Containers can be helpful in workspaces to help organize supplies and to cut down on visual clutter. Consider using baskets or containers on open shelves to hold loose items. Your space will immediately look less busy and more organized. This translates to feeling more grounded.

Square or Rectangle

The shape associated with the Earth element is square or rectangle. The four corners of a square or rectangle lend to it being a stable, reliable, grounding shape. Objects are more stable when they have four legs or four corners, including animals or even a house. Compare this with the dynamism of the three-sided Fire element that creates energy. The Earth element grounds the energy. If you look around your home, you will see that most furnishings are square or rectangular-shaped, including desks, tables, beds, couches, armchairs, coffee tables, and picture frames.

Office Space/Desk

Those dominant in the Earth element may favor the kitchen table as their office given the option. They prefer working with or around groups of people or, better yet, spending time with their family or inner circle, as opposed to working alone in an office away from where the action is. To integrate more Earth into your workday, consider your office location and whether it feels too isolating. If so, situate closer to others to feel part of a team. For purposes of a desk, I suggest a square or rectangle desk for more grounding. Create an office space in which you have both safety and freedom for self-expression. Choose warm lighting to create a cozy space. The more rooted you are, the more expansion you can experience.

Earth Elements for Workspaces
- Baskets
- Pottery
- Organizing containers
- Flowerpots
- Square or rectangular desk or tables
- Terra cotta
- Southwest landscape art
- Southwest motifs
- Couch or armchair

Earth Element Activities

The best way to embody more of the Earth element is simple: be more human. If you're like me, being on planet Earth doesn't always feel like home. In Ram Dass's book *Walking Each Other Home*, he speaks of Earth as a temporary place where we're learning lessons and expanding our soul's evolution until we return to our real home.[35] It's alluring to put our focus somewhere else as a place of refuge rather than our current circumstances. As more of my immediate family members have passed over, I find myself drifting to spiritual dimensions more than I probably should. While it's important to keep in mind that life is bigger than the here and now, in accordance with our religious or spiritual beliefs, we can also veer over into a state of escapism or denial. When we live from a place other than the present moment, we become ungrounded and life on Earth loses its enjoyability.

We could all take a cue from primary Earth elements who know how to enjoy the best of being alive. Earth activities can help us enjoy the physical nature and five senses of being human. It's easy to overlook Earth activities or even resist them if we don't allow ourselves to receive the bounty that Mother Earth has to offer us. You might think it takes too much time to cook, to garden, or to walk in nature. These may seem like time indulgences. Of course, it's these indulgences that also sustain us. When you make time for the Earth element activities, you'll get back in spades in the form of good health, abundance, and happiness.

Cooking

One of the most grounding activities you can do is cooking. Working with fresh vegetables and grains is an immediate way to work with the Earth element. The closer your ingredients come from the land, the more you will experience the benefits. Take a trip to your local farmers market or consider growing some herbs or vegetables at home. As much as I love eating out, there's also nothing better than a home-cooked meal. The smell of olive oil and garlic heating on the stove immediately smells like home. Cooking can feel like a chore since we have to eat multiple times every day. However, consider cooking a gourmet meal out of a cookbook every now and then with fresh ingredients you love. You'll immediately feel more in your body and in the present moment.

Bodywork

The Earth element is the most physical of all the elements and therefore the most present to the moment. In comparison, the Water element can drift off into thought, while the Wood element is planning ahead for the future much of the time, and the Metal element is often thinking about the past and how it can be improved. When the Fire element is focused, she has the ability to be present, but it takes much concentration to maintain. The Earth element, on the other hand, is engaged in the five senses of taste, smell, touch, sight, and hearing to the point where it's hard to ignore what's in their immediate environment.

If the Earth element is your missing element, then consider getting a massage or other bodywork to help you embody more of the physical world. Our body is always in the present moment and when your attention is on it, then you can't help but also be present. This is the reason when we have physical pain, it's difficult to think of anything else. But the same is true when we're experiencing something pleasant.

If you tend to be in your head a lot, then it's time to bring your attention into your body. Physical exercise can help, but even then we can space out with a podcast or other stimulation that takes our mind somewhere else. Physical touch can help bring you down to earth and be more present. Moreover, human touch can have significant health benefits, including a decreased heart rate, lower blood pressure, improved circulatory system, and a reduction of stress hormones.

Make Art

Anytime we use our hands to make something, we come into the present moment. When we're in the present moment engaged with something physical, the Earth element is activated. This includes any art or craft project. Pottery is one of the best Earth element activities one can do. During one of the most stressful times in my life, I found myself taking pottery classes. A friend of mine was a pottery teacher and he suggested I join his class. Not knowing then what I know now, it was the perfect activity to help ground me at a time when I was going through a divorce, changing jobs, and moving. I loved those two hours of throwing clay on the wheel and the glazing process. If you've ever been drawn to making pottery or any other type of art, follow your intuition and enroll in a pottery or art class.

Earth Element Activities
- Cooking and baking
- Breadmaking
- Gardening
- Nature walks
- Pottery
- Craft projects
- Camping

- Dog walking
- Bodywork, such as massage
- Home improvement
- Interacting with children and pets

Earth Element Wardrobe

Those with a prominent Earth element are happy to blend into the background, and their wardrobe helps them do just that. They generally stick with earth tones, monotones, and neutrals. The shape associated with the Earth element is square, and so their clothing may tend toward fitting slightly boxy rather than form fitting. Accessories are worn not for adornment but in association with friends or family members or for practical purposes, such as a watch or necklace with a keepsake attached. Shoes are comfortable, practical, and worn in. Earth elements have an affinity for nature, and so often their wardrobe will reflect this identity.

If you're needing more Earth element, then try dressing cozy, comfortable, and practical every now and then. Take the day off or at least opt to not take Zoom meetings. Schedule a massage or take an art class, and pick up some warm bread and fresh veggies to roast on your way home. Give thanks to Earth for blessing you with its abundance and receive the goodness she has to offer.

Earth Element Worksheet

Earth Element Profile Ranking: _____

(primary, missing, other...)

- ❏ I need *more* of the Earth element.
- ❏ I need *less* of the Earth element.
- ❏ I am balanced in the Earth element.

Insights about the role of the Earth Element in my life and work:

_____

_____

_____

_____

Earth Elements to add to workspace:

_____

_____

_____

Earth Element activities to incorporate:

_____

_____

_____

Earth Elements to include in wardrobe:

_____

_____

_____

Earth Elements to eliminate, if needed:

_____

_____

_____

CHAPTER 11
Pedal to the Metal

> The details are not the details. They make the design.
> —Charles Eames

When I was a kid, one of my favorite things to do after school was to grab my ten-speed and take off as fast as I could through my neighborhood. After being cooped up all day in a classroom, I felt free as I pedaled as fast as I could. It felt like I was going forty miles an hour when it was probably five at best. Occasionally, there were those days when, out of nowhere, a clinking sound began and the pedals no longer worked. The chain had come off the gear shaft. The first couple of times this happened, I had to walk my bike home so my dad could fix it. After watching him a few times, I figured out how to do it myself. That way when it happened, I could continue my freedom tour until it was time to come home for dinner.

No one likes when things go off the rails, when your chain's being yanked, or when there's a crumb in your butter. Details matter. In fact, the longer I live, the more I believe it to be true that the devil's in the details. This well-known adage sums up the Metal phase. Although it's an easily overlooked phase of the Five Elements Cycle, it can make or break a project. The paradox is that the details that feel stifling to you can end up freeing you.

Attention to Detail

People seem to either love or hate the Metal phase. In the creative process, we tend to think more in terms of the yang phases of Wood and Fire, when you put energy into creating something, not extracting energy away from it. But tell that to a sculptor, a film editor, hair stylist, or fashion designer. Their entire job is taking an existing object and culling it down to something better than it was before. There's nothing wrong with a block of wood, but imagine what it could become once a wood carver chips away at it. The same is true for film footage after a day of shooting. It's not until the editor edits it that the story makes sense. And think about a head of hair before a stylist takes hold of it.

These are all examples of a Metal element doing what she does best—taking something and editing it to become an even better version of itself. The same is true for any project. It's not complete, at least in terms of its highest potential, until it goes through the Metal phase. For this reason, many projects get sidelined, abandoned, or don't have the success they could have had when all they needed was the Metal phase. As a book coach, I find this to be especially true. Once a writer finishes the first draft (Fire phase), she often doesn't have the desire or desired ability to edit it in a second draft. As a result, many books get shelved before ever finding their way to print.

You might be thinking you'd rather hire out the Metal element to those who specialize in it, such as an editor, accountant, architect, or designer. After all, we're not expected, nor would it be wise, to draw up the architectural plans for our house, proofread the final draft of our book, or do our own taxes when you can leave it to the professionals. You're absolutely right. And yet there are times when you need to tap into your inner Metal element to finish everyday tasks or complete projects that can only be accomplished with the precision of your unique signature. And sometimes you've got to be the one who puts the chain back on your bike if you want to ride it home.

Our inner Metal element is who keeps track of time, keeps us organized enough to get through the day, and maintains order in our home and work environment. When your Metal element is turned on, you will feel more in control of your life. Things will work better and fall into place easier, and you will find success sooner. For those with a weak or missing Metal element, you might find that you run late for meetings, forget where you place items, or gloss over details that results in unnecessary problems later.

I encourage my writing clients to complete their second draft as much as possible before turning it over to a professional editor. It's the second draft where we can dig deeper into our message or story and find our voice that much more. Unless you work with an experienced editor or ghostwriter who spends a lot of time with you, replicating your voice, message, or expertise is challenging. Any project that's a creation of yours needs your energy in it from start to finish. Of course, collaboration is always a viable option, as discussed in part 3, but know that your unique perspective can't be replaced by anyone.

The more you engage with the Metal element, the better your eye for details. The more I edit my work and others', the more the typos jump off the page. As you work with the Metal element, you'll become more proficient in completing tasks than you ever knew was possible. Who doesn't love checking a box off the to-do list, deleting the last email in your inbox, or a clean kitchen countertop after a big meal? A true Metal element person takes pride in their workspace, which makes it the perfect place to start for adding some Metal into your day.

Adding Metal to Your Workspace

Because the Metal element adds precision, focus, and order to the creative cycle, it can also do this for you and your workspace. For those who prefer a modern, minimal space with clean lines, you're a Metal element at heart and already a step ahead. I've never met anyone who didn't desire organization and order in their spaces. Even if you are an artist who likes to spread out their project and splash paint around, I'm guessing you still prefer knowing there's a place for everything. It is possible to be organized, creative, and messy. Let's start with the baseline of organization.

Metal Element Symbols

Color: Metallics, white, gray, pastels

Shape: Circle or oval

Interiors: Metal hardware, slate, granite, stone

Organization

The Metal element is the quintessential organizer. Chapter 7 discussed the benefits of decluttering in the Water phase as a way to plant new seeds. This is also the case in the Metal phase as the energy becomes more refined before finding completion in the Water phase. You can think of the Metal phase as doing the job of our intestines (which the Metal element rules in Chinese Medicine). The small and large intestines organize food into nutrients and waste just prior to elimination. Think of the Metal element as what separates the wheat from the chaff. You can see what an important function this is with any project. Let's apply that same standard to your workspace.

In Marie Kondo's wildly popular book *The Life-Changing Magic of Tidying Up*, she started a revolution of wielding the Metal element around our home couched in the phrase "Does it spark joy?"[36] As a professional organizer first, Kondo included the decluttering process in her book, making the point that there's no point organizing things that you need to get rid of. I couldn't agree more. It's hard to talk about organizing without including decluttering. Similarly, in editing a book, you declutter it first in the developmental editing stage before you worry about reworking and organizing sentences in the copyediting stage.

Imagine your office as a manuscript. What needs to be edited out to best move the story along? And by story, I mean your work in the world. How can you set up systems to be more efficient? Create systems so that there is a natural inflow and outflow of papers, supplies, or reference materials you use. Of course, this also applies to your online office. As we become acclimated to more cloud and less paper, so much of our organization takes place online with email and cloud storage.

It's important to schedule time on your calendar for setting up the necessary systems for your work, along with periodic maintenance. If you feel unorganized with emails and day-to-day admin work, then it will eventually catch up to you. Seek assistance from a bookkeeper, website designer, or virtual assistant for tasks that seem overwhelming to you or that could be better accomplished by someone who specializes in a particular area. The more order in your space, the more in control you will feel over your work and life. While it may seem like you're taking time away from creating content or other money-generating activities, you're doing the opposite. The more structures you have in place, the more creative you'll be.

Metal Objects

After you've tackled the organization and decluttering of your workspace, you can then add the Metal element to your space. The Metal element, true to its character, gives structure and form to many household furnishings. For example, a metal base is often used to give support to tables, lamps, chairs, windows, and even entire buildings. Metal is also used for decorative purposes in homes. For example, metal art and frames are common. Accenting furniture and art with gold and silver is another way to bring Metal into a space. Also consider mixing in colors associated with the Metal element, which include metallics, white, and pastels. As a Metal element, an all-white room lives up to its reputation as being minimal, clean, and refined.

Crystals and Gemstones

Crystals and gemstones have always been a favorite of those in the healing arts, but they're also popular among interior decorators to use as home accessories. I love bringing the natural world into spaces to bridge nature with the indoors. Crystals and gemstones have so many wonderful properties, physically and metaphysically, that can enhance the energy in spaces. To bring in specific energetic properties to your space, consult a book on crystals or shop intuitively at a gem and mineral shop. Rocks, shells, and sand are Metal elements formed from the Earth element, as are any finishes made of rock, such as granite, slate, and marble.

Desk

The Metal element is symbolically expressed through the shape of a oval or round. For example, a round table would bring in aspects of the Metal element as opposed to an Earth-like square or rectangle table. Most items contain a combination of elements.

For example, a round wood desk would have the properties of the Wood element and Metal element. One of my favorite work surfaces to work on is a round marble desk. It incorporates all the attributes of the Metal element: the round shape, the color white, and the marble slab. This would make a great accent table for those who want to add the Metal element to their space.

For an office desk, an all-metal desk may be too much of the Metal element and create a cold feel. It's no coincidence that filing cabinets, which are the ultimate organizers of paper, are also usually made of metal. Too much metal can cinch creative juices just like a metal filing cabinet can kill a creative buzz. Use in moderation. You might consider a white desk or a wood desk that uses metal as its hardware. A combination of wood with metal hardware is often used in trendy industrial spaces to create a harmonious balance of these two opposing elements. When you combine elements that are oppositional, such as Wood and Metal or Fire and Water, it creates a dynamic look in interior spaces. Keep in mind, however, it's about balance. Too much of a good thing is too much.

Metal Elements for Workspaces
- Metal chair legs
- Metal table bases
- Wall clocks
- Metal art and frames
- Shells
- Salt lamps
- Wrought-iron railing
- Crystals and gemstones
- Appliances
- Copper, aluminum, and gold accents

- Granite and slate countertops
- Marble and stone finishes
- Concrete

Metal Element Activities

The best way to get better at anything is by practice. This is certainly the case for Metal element attributes. Whether one has discipline to see a project through will expose itself at the Metal element phase of the creative cycle. This technical, detailed, and focused phase can be challenging to our twenty-first-century minds filled with distraction and attention-deficit tendencies from so much stimulation coming at us from all directions. However, with practice you too can hone your mind to become more focused.

The Metal element traits are often the most challenging to flowy Water folks, along with Wood and Fire types who would rather look at the big picture and are more likely to adopt the adage "Go big or go home." However, to be more effective, their ideas and projects need the precision and refinement that the Metal element provides. The Metal element is an underestimated energy that brings a sense of control to creative projects. It can often be frowned upon, or misrepresented, because it can easily trigger our inner critic. When the Metal element is in balance, however, it helps us with constructive critique rather than criticism.

Cleaning

Your space is a reflection of your mental state and vice versa. Therefore, by engaging in Metal activities, you can start to access your inner Metal element in a healthy, balanced way, as opposed to it showing up disguised as your inner critic. In addition to decluttering and organizing, one of the simplest ways to access the Metal element is cleaning. I recommend this step after a round of decluttering to give your space a fresh start. When you take control over your space, you will have a sense of more control over your life. You will gain so much more energy and clarity to tackle your work projects and your space will feel so much better too.

Creative Arts

The Metal element activities don't require the same vigor as discussed with the Wood and Fire elements. Instead, the Metal activities are about detail and precision and require an element of control to be relatively successful. For example, playing classical piano, video editing, woodworking, fashion design, and technical drawing engage our ability to focus. They have a certain quality of organization and control that's unique compared to other creative arts. It's no wonder that the best interior designers and architects are Metal elements. You could equate those with a strong aesthetic and attention to detail to Virgos in Western astrology. For example, interior designer Nate Berkus prides himself as being #doublevirgo on Instagram, and it shows in his refined taste in interior selections.

Metal Element Activities

- Organizing and decluttering
- Cleaning (home or car)
- Technical drawing
- Book editing
- Framing and matting pictures
- Photo or video editing
- Classical piano
- Landscaping

- Coding
- Martial arts
- Space planning
- Vipassana (one-pointed) meditation
- Selecting interior finishes
- Organizing (or deleting) photos
- Woodworking
- Self-care practices, such as nails, grooming

Metal Element Wardrobe

As you've likely noticed by now, each element stays consistent with its characteristics whether it is a personality trait, an activity, or an outfit. Likewise, you can probably guess that the wardrobe of a primary Metal element is simple, well-tailored, and neatly put together. Metal elements lean toward whites and grays and will throw in some metallics or pastels every now and then. They will accessorize but with much intention: for example, with a statement bracelet or designer watch. Shoes are polished, high-end leather, stylish, and efficient.

On days you need to access your Metal element, consider dressing like a Metal element. Opt for solids rather than patterns. Don't eliminate but reduce your accessories, except those that are essential, such as a watch and your wedding band. If you really want to make a Metal element statement that says you have your pedal to the metal, then iron your clothes, get a manicure, and shine your shoes.

Metal Element Worksheet

Metal Element Profile Ranking: _____

(primary, missing, other…)

- ❑ I need *more* of the Metal element.
- ❑ I need *less* of the Metal element.
- ❑ I am balanced in the Metal element.

Insights about the role of the Metal Element in my life and work:

_____

_____

_____

_____

Metal Elements to add to workspace:

_____

_____

_____

Metal Element activities to incorporate:

_____

_____

_____

Metal Elements to include in wardrobe:

_____

_____

_____

Metal Elements to eliminate, if needed:

_____

_____

_____

PART 3
Integrating the Five Elements with Other People

CHAPTER 12

Creating Collaboration

Great collaboration feels like playing jazz.
—Ray Dalio, *Principles*

In part 2, you learned how to access and integrate all Five Elements to become a whole and complete version of yourself. In embracing your missing element, you make amends and perhaps even friends with your shadow. No longer do you need to cringe or altogether avoid situations in which your missing element presents itself. You'll now have a choice to go into your weak element knowing this is not the monster it was before or choose to collaborate with others as you'll learn in this chapter. Either way, you have choices about how you navigate your way through all five phases of the creative process.

In Taoist principles, we are all made up of the same elements with the only variable being our constitution of those five elements. We incarnate for the purpose to experience individuation, and yet our ultimate lesson is that we're all drops of the same ocean. There are times to go it alone for purposes of putting our unique stamp onto something. But we're also here to partner, to collaborate, and to be part of something bigger than ourselves. We can create solo, but there's also a time to create with others.

We can make a product or service as a solo entrepreneur, or we can choose to scale it bigger with more people through a corporation, or we can settle in between with a partnership. We are here for individual expression, but we're also here to merge with others for a variety of purposes depending on our unique path.

We are social beings with many different types of relationships, including spouses, coworkers, children, business partners, and neighbors. Some of these relationships are voluntary, while others seem forced upon us, as in the case of neighbors and coworkers. However, everyone who comes into our life is a projection of aspects within ourselves with whom we must coexist. Whatever is not balanced within ourselves we will unconsciously seek out in others.

You've most likely experienced a spectrum of personal and professional relationships that ran the gamut from triggering to simpatico to passionate. In hindsight, you can see how you grew from all experiences. The triggering relationship might start out as a strong attraction or repulsion, while the passionate relationship may feel as if the other person completes you in some way. It's usually not until we resolve the trigger that we move on from the triggering relationship, or else we will attract the same underlying trait in someone else. Some relationships feel like sandpaper, while others are effortlessly harmonious. Our soul's path gives us both types of relationships to work out our rough edges while also giving us free passes. In both, we expand.

It's no wonder the phrase "You are the yin to my yang" is so common—this is exactly what's happening upon meeting someone who fills in your missing element. There is a magnetic pull as our internal elements strive toward balance. We are attracted to those people who have the element(s) that we don't have or, better yet, who have the element we have but haven't fully accessed within ourselves. We are only attracted to what and who we know ourselves to be.

You may notice that you find yourself attracted, personally or platonically, to a certain type of person. For example, I work best with Fire elements. I love their enthusiasm and the energy they put toward whatever their passionate about in the moment. You may notice a pattern in people you've dated or married and the energy qualities they have in common. This will give you a clue to what your missing element is and, thus, your hidden strength.

You may notice that it's those same people who, after some time together, trigger you. When the attraction within a relationship is based on our deficiencies, you will inevitably encounter challenges, unless it is an agreed-upon exchange in the case of a business relationship. By integrating our missing element for which the other person provided us the energy, the relationship will change. It will either become obsolete, no longer stimulating, or possibly more harmonious.

Now consider a relationship based not upon filling in each other's weaknesses but exploiting each other's strengths. It's a slight variation in perspective but significant. Let's use the dynamic duo of Elton John and his long-time writing partner Bernie Taupin as an example. It's not that Elton John couldn't write songs or that Bernie Taupin couldn't perform. Instead, Elton John's strength is performance and Bernie Taupin's strength is writing lyrics. Not surprisingly, Taupin is multitalented in a number of other ways, including producing, recording his own albums, poetry, and even small acting roles. He could have been successful in many ways but clearly found his collaboration with Elton John to be the highest expression of his talents.

In an interview for *Rolling Stones* magazine, Taupin remarked, "I couldn't live [Elton's] life. I would rather drill myself in the head with a nail gun than do what he does."[37] Clearly, Elton John also found his own successes doing what he does best. The point is neither Elton John nor Bernie Taupin was dependent on the other, and instead they allowed each to play to their strengths, resulting in epic successes.

None of us would be here without collaboration, even if it were only for a moment in time. We are the third, the creation, formed through a collaboration of two people. From there, we collaborate and create more thirds. This is the essence of the universal flower of life symbol that exemplifies expansion and abundance of life energy. In his book *Principles*, Ray Dalio writes, "Two people who collaborate well will be about three times as effective as each of them operating independently, because each will see what the other might miss—plus they can leverage each other's strengths while holding each other accountable to higher standards."[38]

When a collaboration is harmonious, it exceeds what any one person can do on his own. When not harmonious, however, it can end disastrously. Far more business partnerships fail rather than enjoy the successes as did Elton and Bernie, Ben and Jerry, or Ray and Charles Eames. In fact, statistics show that approximately 70 percent of partnerships fail.[39] An *Inc.* magazine article provided three tips for creating a successful partnership, with the first being to "look for partners who fill in gaps." Trust between partners was second on the list, and the third recommendation was to partner with someone who is "collaborative and growth-oriented," with growth referring to someone who is "in a constant process of improving."[40] This sums up our goal of using the Five Elements as our guide: partner with those who can help fill in your missing element, but also continue to expand and grow yourself.

While there's no formula on chemistry between people, we can predict to a certain degree how the elements will react to one another by looking at how the elements respond to one another in nature. We are no different, except that we add consciousness to the equation. We can ultimately find harmony with another when we approach it from the mindset of win-win-win—that is, a win for me, a win for you, and a win for the planet. In relationships with friction, we can work together to discover one another's strengths to smooth out the edges and create more harmony.

The following sections provide the likely synergy between the elements in personal relationships or business collaborations based on one's primary element. When we collaborate, we naturally lead with what we're best at—in other words, our primary element. And when the other person comes to the table with their best self, then the two can create something better than the two could have on their own. In my example of Elton John and Bernie Taupin, Elton's primary element is the Fire element, evident by his flashy outfits and outgoing stage presence, while Bernie Taupin's primary element is the more refined Metal element, who finds the perfect song lyrics and prefers to be behind the scenes. The Fire and Metal element collaboration is one of the best for manifesting and completing successful projects.

As you read about the following collaborations, consider them in terms of your primary element and how you collaborate with other element types. Also consider how the two elements mix within your own constitution. For example, if you scored highest in Wood and Fire, then notice how these two energies act in concert together. You might notice some harmonious aspects about yourself or possibly paradoxical aspects about yourself that now makes sense in light of your Five Elements profile. Let's start with the Water element, who might be the most reluctant to collaborate but can also gain the most through working with others.

Water Collaborations

As the most introverted of the Five Elements, the Water element has little desire to go outside its bubble, and yet it can do a world of good to do so. The Water element can be mistaken as being shy or even aloof at times. However, it's not so much their desire to be alone as it is their relationship to the spiritual realm that takes them out of the daily routines of earthly life. But when they emerge from the depths of their psyche, they enjoy relating to others, preferably those with depth. Let's look at how the Water element interacts with the other elements.

Water and Water

SOS! With two Water elements you might need to throw in the life preservers to rescue them from the depths of the insular world they've created. These two loners would most likely love working from home, all while discovering a cure for a pandemic and ending world hunger as well. The problem, however, is that no one would ever find out about it. Neither have social media accounts or a desire to profit off their gifts. At death, their beneficiaries will find papers and files full of their work never published. Suffice it to say, these two would be happy as clams together. Beyond that, however, they might consider partnering with other element types to expand their world and reach an audience with their creations.

Water and Wood

These two go together like peas and carrots. There's an ease and synergy between them that's supportive for both elements. In the Five Elements Cycle, the Water element gives energy to the Wood element for purposes of growth and expansion. In terms of relationships, the Water element pours onto the Wood element a wellspring of ideas and inspiration without effort. The Water element is seen in this relationship for her value that might not otherwise get recognition from other element types. In exchange, the Wood element builds on the inspiration from the Water element and makes something tangible from it. It is a win-win relationship.

For more information, see the *Wood and Water* section.

Water and Fire

The phrases "You complete me" and "You are the yin to my yang" may have been first coined by a Water and Fire couple. These two bring out the best in each other and literally complete the missing element within themselves. The Water element brings the calm back into the Fire element's life to help refuel, while the Fire element gives the Water element the spark it needs to come out of its shell. Together, they can create steam. Where they differ, however, is in their energy levels, which can require a compromise when it comes to activities and social outings.

For more information, see the *Fire and Water* section.

Water and Earth

Controlling much? That's how the Water element may feel in relationship with the Earth element. In the Five Elements Cycle, Earth contains Water. Think of how destructive water can be when it's not contained. Floods completely take over cities and homes when left to their own devices, hence the need for dams, plumbing, or even a cup to drink from. Water doesn't like to be contained. If it weren't for the Earth element, we'd have no way of effectively utilizing the Water element. This describes these two elements in relationship. Water doesn't like to be contained by the smothering Earth element, and yet the only way the gifts of the Water element can be used for practical purposes is by containing it in some way. This is truly a karmic relationship in which each needs to understand its role in the other's life. And when that's accomplished, the world benefits and our cup runneth over with its gifts.

For more information, see the *Earth and Water* section.

Water and Metal

You know you're in the company of someone special to you when you can be comfortable in silence together. This is the case with the Water and Metal element. These two yin elements feel familiar to one another. Both are independent thinkers not expecting much from the other. If these two elements work together, then the Metal element will be tech support and all things practical, while the Water element is the idea person. In personal relationships, both enjoy a slower pace of life and are content with a minimal lifestyle. If there is a complaint, it's that each is looking to the other for taking the initiative on making decisions or taking action.

For more information, see the *Metal and Water* section.

Wood Collaborations

Those dominant in the Wood element are independent and can sometimes take the path of the lone wolf. If so, it's not because they don't enjoy the company of others, but because few others see the big vision they see or are willing to take action on it. However, it's important for the Wood element to also know when to work in partnership or with a team. The Wood element can sometimes take on a jack-of-all-trades identity because they have a knowledge base in a large range of topics due to their unending need to learn and seek new things. As a result, they tend to have a lot of projects going on at the same time. Finishing those projects, however, is another skillset that they could improve upon through collaboration. Let's look at the different ways in which a primary Wood element mixes with the other elements.

Wood and Wood

When two Wood elements put their heads together, there's no lack of ideas. These two are ready to take on the world together and will take action steps in doing so. But how far they get from the start line is the real test. When two people with the same primary element pair up, it feels like immediate chemistry. *The Wood element in me sees the Wood element in you.* It can be an enjoyable relationship with good communication, but if the project starts to stall, it's time to bring another element into the mix. For two Wood elements, try adding your wood energy to a Fire element to get your project cooking. Be mindful to build enough grounding with the Earth element to get things off the ground so that they can really take off.

Wood and Water

The Wood and Water elements are highly compatible. Being next to each other in the creative cycle, these two are simpatico, as the Water element feeds the Wood with ideas and the Wood element takes action that the Water element might not otherwise have the gumption to take. Where the Water element ends and the Wood element begins is not always clear with these two elements because of their harmonious nature. When it comes to presenting their ideas, however, the Wood element is certain to take the lead and be the spokesperson.

In personal relationships, these two can brainstorm ideas all day long. The Wood element may focus on work and career more so than the Water element, but they have plenty in common after work. For example, when watching a movie, the Water element enjoys a quiet evening at home, while the Wood element watches the movie from the lens of a cinematographer or director. The Wood element is the more extroverted of the two, while the Water element is quieter at least in social situations.

For Water elements who have low energy or are challenged with depression, pairing with a Wood element can help them grow. That being said, it's important that the Wood element continues to expand and evolve in the world and not become too soggy. Water is essential to a plant's growth, but too much over-saturates it and eventually stalls its growth.

For more information, see the *Water and Wood* section.

Wood and Fire

The pairing of the Wood and Fire elements is truly a dynamic duo. With these two yang elements, the world is their oyster. The Wood element sparks the idea and the Fire element takes up the reins and gives it the necessary passion it needs to keep it moving along. The Wood element needs the excitement and encouragement that comes so naturally for the Fire element to give. The Fire element gives the Wood element the validation it needs to keep going. The Fire element will appear to be the dominant energy of the two because her high energy naturally attracts the spotlight. The Wood element takes on a management role of sorts while the Fire element continues to build the requisite energy needed to keep the ball rolling. For example, in a fundraising situation, it would be the Fire element in front of the camera while the Wood element is in charge behind the scenes, taking care of business.

In personal relationships, these two have a lot of fun together. Social outings and family life are a point of compatibility, although the Fire element tends to scatter her energy more so than the Wood element. Because the Fire element, in general, is the highest expression of energy, when it expresses itself through a person, it doesn't always understand the word *no*. The Fire element is a *yes* person, whereas the Wood element is a *yes, maybe* person. As a result, there could be conflicts with apportionment of time and energy. However, overall, these two have more in common than not and can accomplish a lot together.

For more information, see the *Fire and Wood* section.

Wood and Earth

The combination of Wood and Earth offers a lot of opportunity for growth. It's not the easiest of pairings, but once there is an understanding of what each can offer the other, it can be an incredibly supportive relationship. The wide-eyed Wood element can feel held down or controlled by the Earth element. Meanwhile, the Earth element can feel like the Wood is unreliable and destabilizing to its otherwise peaceful life. Wood seeks change and exploration, while Earth seeks status quo and comfort. Their priorities are polar opposite, and yet they each need the energy of the other for purposes of their own growth.

At work, the Earth element can feel like the micromanaging boss. In personal relationships, the Wood element may feel like she's being controlled or that her dreams are being tamped down by the Earth element. However, when these two realize that they can support the growth of the other, then they are a formidable pair that can experience lots of soul growth. You could call this a karmic relationship in which each has something to learn from the other, and thus, it is challenging but for a purpose.

The Wood element needs the Earth element to keep its plans realistic and grounded. For example, when I told my Earth element mother that I was moving to California, her nest was shaken. She questioned my plans and thought I was crazy. As the pioneer-minded Wood element, I plowed forward with my plans. However, there were some snags that I hadn't thought through. As I began to fill in the details, she came around to the idea. The truth is the idea was scary to me too, and it was knowing that I would be coming home to visit on a regular basis that grounded me into this big change.

The Earth element also needs the Wood element to keep it moving and not get stuck in a rut. Without Wood, the ground lacks movement. When the Wood person is more grounded in her plans and the Earth person is more open to change, then these two can find mutual respect. As a result of my move, I had the opportunity to spend significant time with my parents when I came home for visits. They enjoyed hearing about what was happening in my life, while I got to enjoy the benefits of feeling at home. And there's no better home than that of the Earth element.

For more information, see the *Earth and Wood* section.

Wood and Metal

Like the Wood and Earth combo, this relationship can also be strained until and unless each can appreciate the other's role. In the Five Elements Cycle, the Metal element controls the Wood element, and this is exactly what it feels like in a relationship between these two. The Wood element may feel its wings being clipped with the Metal element constantly finding flaws in its grand plans. This is true in love or at work. However, the Wood element must realize that there's truth in what the Metal element suggests. When in balance, the Metal element only makes projects better. If out of balance, however, the Metal element can be controlling or tunnel visioned. The Metal element communicates directly and literally, to the point of being blunt. It's important for the Wood element not to confuse the Metal element's communication as being critical, and also for the Metal element to soften his approach for more harmony within the relationship.

The short-term desires of the Wood element and the Metal element are opposite of one another: the Wood element seeks growth and expansion, while the Metal element wants minimalism and precision. The key, however, is to keep the larger goal in mind. Both want success of whatever is at stake, whether it's a vacation, a dinner party, a film production, or the launch of a book. Without the Wood element, the Metal element would get lost in the woods for lack of seeing the forest. Without the Metal element, the Wood element might find completion of the project, but it won't reach the same success it would have but for the fine tuning of the Metal element. When you put these elements together in harmonious balance, you get a visionary project (Wood) with a strong foundation (Earth) that meets the necessary feasibility tests (Metal). You get success.

For more information, see the *Metal and Wood* section.

Fire Collaborations

Those with a primary Fire element love collaboration, whether one-on-one or in groups. As Fire is the most outgoing of all elements, relationships are their highest priority and also where they shine the most. Notwithstanding, Fire elements still need their refuge away from people to recharge their batteries. Pairing with others can help them do just that, particularly the yin elements, Water and Metal. Let's look at how the Fire element interacts with all the elements:

Fire and Fire

If there were ever too much of a good thing, it might be two Fire elements in collaboration. This duo may be too hot to handle for their own good. Because both are used to being the center of attention, competition or conflicts could arise as each seeks taking the stage. That being said, they share the same vigor toward life and can have lots of fun together. They generate a lot of enthusiasm for others, but productivity is unlikely unless they can bring other elements into their lively mix.

It's rare to see two Fire elements in marriage unless both have integrated the other elements. If so, then they can be an electric power couple. We usually find that opposites attract in love relationships. You may have observed in your own relationship or others that one partner is extremely outgoing and the other is more introverted. Love relationships are the primary way we find balance of the elements and thus why we often pair with someone with a different primary element. Within a family unit, children also play a role in filling in the Five Element balance within a household.

Fire and Water

If opposites attracting is the key to relationships, then this pair has what it takes. The Fire element is the most yang and the Water element is the most yin, making them the most opposite of all the Five Element collaborations. With the Fire element being so energetic, you might think it would be the dominant one in the relationship, but the reality is that Water controls Fire in the Five Elements Cycle. This means that the Water element can pour water on the Fire element when it wants. This could go one of two ways: soggy or steamy.

For example, if the Water element insists on staying in on the weekend while the Fire element needs more social outlets, compatibility issues could arise. However, if the Fire element needs someone to keep them in check with overextending their energy, then the Water element can be the perfect person to do just that. Maybe a quiet dinner at home by candlelight is just what the doctor ordered the Fire element. It's a delicate balance. If the Water element splashes too much Water on the Fire's flames, then resentment could creep into the relationship.

For more information, see the *Water and Fire* section.

Fire and Wood

These two yang elements are the Thelma and Louise of all pairings. They are compatible, perhaps even combustible, with the Wood element being the initiator and the Fire element being the manifester. Fire loves Wood's ideas and Wood loves the enthusiasm that Fire adds. This is a great combination full of Fire energy and Wood practicality that can go the distance.

For more information, see the *Wood and Fire* section.

Fire and Earth

The combination of these two elements is like being at home with a roaring fire in the hearth. It's warm, cozy, while also being fun and exciting. Fire creates Earth in the Five Elements cycle but only after exhausting itself in the Fire phase. That's the dynamic between these two elements in a relationship. The Fire element loves coming home to the Earth element after a long day. Likewise, the Earth element enjoys the excitement that the Fire element provides.

In relationships, the Earth element may end up in a caretaking role for the Fire element. If this is an agreed-upon arrangement, then the two can have a harmonious relationship. However, if the Earth element is out of balance with herself, then she can feel self-sacrificing without her own needs being met. In work matters, the two work quite well together, with each taking on very different roles that support one another. The Earth element will always opt for a supporting role, holding space for the Fire element to do what she does best: shine brightly.

For more information, see the *Earth and Fire* section.

Fire and Metal

We often attract who we need into our life, instead of who we think we want. This is the case with the Fire and Metal elements. The Fire element doesn't know how much he needs a Metal element in his life until he appears. In the Five Elements Cycle, the Fire element controls the Metal element. Think of a metal worker with a flaming torch shaping metal to his liking. Hence, you can imagine there can be some tension in this relationship, unless you think about the possibility that metal wants to be bent and Fire needs to do something to focus its energy. In other words, when you see how each benefits the other, it's not only a harmonious relationship but also a productive and successful one.

Although the Fire element is technically the controlling element of Metal in the Five Elements Cycle, it can seem the other way around in relationships. The yin energy of the Metal element can diminish the Fire element's energy. However, when the Fire element can see that it's for the purpose of creating something more refined and beautiful, then a mutual respect results.

When these two elements come together in collaboration, it can be for a specific soul purpose. Once the kinks are worked out of the relationship, personally or professionally, they can create and manifest beautiful things together.

For more information, see the *Metal and Fire* section.

Earth Collaborations

As the quintessential nurturer of the Five Elements, the Earth element naturally takes on a caretaking role in all relationships, including coworkers, friends, family, or partners. The Earth element is a collaborator by heart, whether it's in terms of family or work. They are the support people behind the scenes who do a lot of the work with little of the credit. They are the glue that keeps all the other elements together and often go unnoticed for the work they do. If this sounds like most moms, you're right. The Earth element is the mother archetype with or without children. Let's look at how the Earth element shows up in her collaboration with the other element types.

Earth and Earth

Two peas in a pod best describes this partnership. This relationship is based on comfort and contentment rather than exploration and expansion. I was once in relationship with a fellow Cancer sign. Although Cancer signs aren't necessarily Earth elements, they share many of the same appreciations as Earth elements, with comfort and security being top priorities. It was the easiest, most harmonious relationship I've ever had. The only reason the relationship didn't continue was because it lacked the ability to grow and evolve beyond the comforts of home. This too is the challenge for two Earth elements. If both parties are content with the status quo, then this duo is in it for the long haul.

Earth and Water

As mentioned in the *Water and Earth* section, this relationship can be contentious. It's important that each realizes the importance they play for each other. When that happens, there can be mutual respect, with each giving the other something they can't find success without. As the Earth element learns to relax into going with the flow and the Water element learns that there is benefit to structure, these two can create beautifully together. Instead of mud, think of these two together as a piece of pottery formed from adding water to clay, molded and sculpted together, to form something beautiful and functional. This is the image to keep in mind if the relationship starts to feel "stuck in a muck" with no forward motion.

For more information, see the *Water and Earth* section.

Earth and Wood

The relationship between the Earth element and Wood element can be supportive if each person is willing to acknowledge the gifts of the other. They each have something the other needs. Earth provides the necessary grounding for Wood, and Wood shakes Earth out of its comfort zone. If Earth gives Wood the space to expand and grow and the Wood element gives the Earth element assurance of its loyalty, then it will be a compatible relationship. Each holds the missing element of the other, and if they can learn from the other to integrate their missing element, then they will have much growth from this relationship. In fact, these two may be soulmates who are here for each other's soul expansion.

For more information, see the *Wood and Earth* section.

Earth and Fire

These two know how to keep the home fires burning. The Earth element and Fire element form a great partnership in love or business. The Earth element gives the Fire element a place to rest while the Fire element gives the Earth element an extra boost of energy and passion for life. The Fire element can get the Earth element out of its rut without too much convincing on the part of the Fire element. An ideal night for these two would be salsa dancing together in the kitchen. At work, the Earth element can be a great support system for the Fire element while the Earth element feels the appreciation reciprocated.

For more information, see the *Fire and Earth* section.

Earth and Metal

The Earth and Metal elements are compatible and easygoing and enjoy each other's company. Although they may not have the passion that Earth and Fire enjoy, they can have a mutually respected friendship that can be long-lasting. The Metal element is formed from the Earth element in the same way sand is a by-product of rock. This process takes place over thousands of years, and so it's unclear exactly when Earth becomes Metal. So is the case with this relationship. There are more similarities than differences to where they can practically read each other's mind, or at least the right arm knows what the left arm is doing. As a result, this can be an extremely productive work relationship and harmonious love partnership.

For more information, see the *Metal and Earth* section.

Metal Collaborations

If you want something done right, ask a Metal element to do it. Their attention to detail can be either a godsend or your worst nightmare. Those sensitive to critique could take offense to the tact delivery of the Metal element. However, if your ego is in check, then you appreciate the efficiency of the Metal element's matter-of-fact approach. They thrive on communicating with precision and have an eye for detail at the expense of seeing the bigger picture. Being slightly introverted, they enjoy the energy of the yang elements as well as the quieter elements. Being more analytical than emotional, they can be hard to read at times, but you can trust they will always tell you the truth when they do speak. Here's how the Metal element interacts with other elements.

Metal and Metal

With two Metal elements in collaboration, you could expect a well-oiled machine regardless of it being at home or in the office. These two could create incredibly efficient systems at home or in a business, that is, if they can agree on who's system is the correct one. A battle of the heads could result where there is no agreeing to disagree. However, if they can agree on the rules of engagement and get on the same page, then they can accomplish a lot together. This is a relationship based more on mind than emotions. Unless spreadsheets are a turn-on, then this romantic relationship may not have the friction it needs to create a spark. However, Metal elements have the ability to build a rocket ship together and blast off to the moon, where they can live happily ever after.

Metal and Water

These two yin elements are both quiet and keep to themselves, except for when in collaboration with other elements. Together, they work great independently. In other words, they can coexist harmoniously, enjoying the company of the other while each doing their own thing. This makes it ideal for working from home if each is given their own space. They are best as coworkers or as partners with each having their own independent lives.

For more information, see the *Water and Metal* section.

Metal and Wood

In feng shui, this relationship is often exemplified as an ax chopping down a tree or pruners pruning a tree. In other words, the dynamic between these two can be seen on a spectrum from extreme chopping to more subtle pruning with the Metal element in the controlling position. It can be a tricky dynamic if the Wood takes the Metal element's words as criticism or if the Metal element takes a hacksaw to the Wood element's plan. But when these two elements work together, it can form a beautiful topiary garden that only these two can create together.

For more information, see the *Wood and Metal* section.

Metal and Fire

These two have the spark that other partnerships seek. They are the perfect mix of focused passion—that is, harnessing one's passionate energy toward creating something amazing. The Metal element helps the Fire element use her laser focus that she otherwise struggles to find on her own. So long as the Fire element can appreciate the taming of its energy, this duo is dynamic.

For more information, see the *Fire and Metal* section.

Metal and Earth

These two have enough in common that they understand each other and enough differences to make things interesting. Earth feels safe with the predictable nature of the Metal element and the Metal element's quirky nature feels seen by the Earth element. They may lack the movement necessary to initiate projects together, but they can give the grounding and structure to that of others. It would be best for these two to integrate more yang energy within themselves or partner with a Wood or Fire element to help create more energy.

For more information, see the *Earth and Metal* section.

★ ★ ★

You now have a better idea how you can partner with other elements to create something you otherwise might not be able to do on your own. Keep in mind, your elemental constitution can evolve over time, and so how you interact with other elements will change accordingly. As you integrate more of your missing element, then how you partner with others will also change. Instead of looking to others to complete you, you will partner with others to accentuate the best of you. This same dynamic is also true in teams and the role we play within a team. Let's now look at how you can create your own dream team.

CHAPTER 13

Creating Your Dream Team

> I define a leader as anyone who takes responsibility
> for finding the potential in people and processes, and
> who has the courage to develop that potential.
>
> —Brené Brown, *Dare to Lead*

The 1992 United States men's basketball team became known as the Dream Team because it was the first time an Olympic team was formed with actively professional players. It was made up of the biggest basketball stars of that time, including Michael Jordon and Scottie Pippen. Selecting from superstars of the NBA, the selection committee chose the best player (plus second string) for each of the five positions. The team went on to win the gold medal after clobbering most of their opponents by over forty points.

A basketball team is made up of the following five players: the center, power forward, small forward, point guard, and shooting guard. Each one of these positions is a metaphor for each of the Five Elements. The 1992 Dream Team exemplifies the Five Elements Cycle. When each player plays his position in accord with the other players, you've got a good team. When each player plays at his highest potential in coordination with the other players, you've got a Dream Team. This is the perfect model for any successful team.

The Role of Each Element in Groups

You now know the characteristics of each of the elements, but how does that element behave in a group dynamic? When we show up in a group dynamic, we usually lead with our primary element. This is what we're naturally good at, and when working with others, we typically want to show up as our best selves. When we're able to fill the role within a group that best fits our primary element, not only is there more individual satisfaction among the members, but the group is more successful at reaching its goal.

Let's look at how each element can best contribute to a group dynamic. In reading each element, consider your primary element and how you can best contribute to a group. The following information can also be useful for managers in hiring and forming teams.

Water Element in Groups

As you know by now, the Water element is the quiet one in the group. However, it's best to use this character trait to the group's advantage. The Water element will be the best listener of the group and will be able to see the bigger vision of the project at hand. Don't expect a Water element to take the lead. Instead, it's best to assign the Water a task that they can do on their own and then report back to the group. This could be in the form of research, writing, or putting together slides for a presentation (for someone else to present). The Water element may not insert herself into group discussions, but that doesn't mean she doesn't have an opinion or a brilliant idea to contribute. Ask a Water element for their thoughts and you might just solve all your problems in doing so.

Wood Element in Groups

The Wood element is a natural initiator of projects and, in fact, may be the project manager or designated leader for the group. If not, the Wood element is able to pivot and take on a quieter role where he works in the background of the group. The Wood element performs best when he is integral to moving a project forward or literally on the move, such as attending meetings or tending to logistics outside of the office. After all, the Wood element is a pioneer at heart and wants to explore new lands, which may be in the form of ideas, strategies, or implementations. The Wood element is self-motivated, doesn't need managing, and best when delegating rather doing everything himself. It's best not to micromanage a Wood element, as it will likely lead a Wood element to move along altogether.

Fire Element in Groups

If the Wood element isn't the leader of the group, then it's likely the Fire element. The Fire element is the most extroverted of the elements, which results in also being seen the most within a group. If the squeaky wheel gets the grease, then the Fire element gets to be seen and heard the most within the group. This is to the group's advantage when it comes to presentations, recruitment, fundraising, outreach, and social networking opportunities. The Fire element is best utilized within a group when having fun doing what he or she enjoys doing. Her enthusiasm is contagious to those within and outside the group. It's best not to assign organizational tasks of the group to the Fire element and instead rely on their people skills.

Earth Element in Groups

The Earth element may be the most understated member of a group, whose participation is integral to the group's success. The Earth element would be equivalent to the center position on a basketball team. This is the person who grounds the team and keeps the members working together as a harmonious unit. The Earth element is the most native to being a true team player and works best when working directly with other team members on projects. If they are sent to do individual tasks, they're likely to come back with a box of donuts or round of lattes for everyone. While the Fire element does best at reaching people outside the group on behalf of the group, the Earth element does best when working within the group. In meetings or strategy sessions, the Earth element will help the group achieve harmony if disagreements or an imbalance arises among its members.

Metal Element in Groups

As the organizer and taskmaster of the group, the Metal element is essential to the success of a group. Although the Metal element lacks the bravado of the Fire element, she can lead a group because of her excellent ability to keep things on track. However, being in the position of leadership isn't what the Metal element usually prefers. Like the Water element, the Metal element is more introverted and prefers working solo for the benefit of the team. It's best to assign the Metal element with tasks that require precision and a deadline. The Metal element will likely not volunteer to lead a group but may emerge as a leader over time as a result of their attention to detail and ability to accomplish tasks in a timely manner, proving that the best leaders can be the quietest ones in the room.

The Power of Five

In the mystical science of numerology, each number, one through nine, is associated with an energy with its own unique characteristics. The number five is the most active of all the numbers. It sits at the midway point, making it the changemaker in numerology. It's no coincidence that the Five Elements Cycle is the process of change that was first revealed in the *I Ching*, which translates to "The Book of Changes." When I see the number sequence 555, I know that it's the resonance for change coming within the next few days.

The number three is also an energetic number. Like the triangle symbol for the Fire element, it holds the same fiery, dynamic qualities. You'll notice that groups of three or five people take on a dynamic quality with the group of five being the most likely to effect change. In his book *Principles*, the billionaire hedge fund investor Ray Dalio, wrote, "Three to five smart, conceptual people seeking the right answers in an open-minded way will generally lead to the best answers. ... Beyond that, adding people actually subtracts from effectiveness."[41]

The number of people in a group makes a difference in its effect and output, with three to five people being the sweet spot. Of course, a group of four can also be fabulous, as the Beatles showed us. Let's look at the different characteristics for groups of three, four, and five people and how to take advantage of each.

Groups of Three People

From age four through our teens, my best friend lived across the street. The two of us spent a lot of time together. After a while, I started to notice the difference between when the two of us would hang out and when another friend would join in. When it was just the two of us, we would have deeper, more intimate conversations, the kind you only have with your best friend. The energy could be low on days when one or both of us were feeling moody. When there were three of us, it was much livelier. If there was trouble to get into, we would find it. The three of us would have so much fun, but it wasn't a time for deep conversations (unless it was about how to get out of trouble with our parents). This is the energy of the group of three people, socially or professionally.

A group of three people will bring energy to any project. How much will get done beyond deciding on happy hour, though, is to be determined. If you're looking to bring enthusiasm and energy to a project, then assemble a group of three people. It's best to have at least one Wood element or one Fire element to stimulate the group and an Earth element to help ground the group if productivity is desired. In well-known groups of three, you'll notice that each person has a different personality type, or element type. Like a tripod, balance can be achieved with three people, but not in the same stable way it can with four people.

Famous groups of three include Janet, Chrissy, and Jack from *Three's Company*; the Three Musketeers; Charlie's Angels; the Three Stooges; the Three Amigos; and Harry, Ron, and Hermione from Harry Potter.

Groups of Four People

If productivity and stability is your goal, then assemble a group of four people. The fab four will get the job done efficiently. The number four in numerology is the most grounded and hardworking of all the numbers. Like a table with four legs or a house with four corners, you can count on it being solid and secure. This is the same energy of the Earth element, which is represented symbolically as a square or rectangle. While the group of three is going to find fun and adventure, the group of four is going to be a reliable foursome that finds practical solutions to everyday challenges. Trust this group to get the job done in a true teamwork fashion.

Like in the group of three people, it's best to vary the elements represented. For example, placing three or four people of the same primary element will not be as productive as having a variety of elements grouped together. According to Dalio in *Principles*, managers should consider "the quality of the people and the differences of the perspectives that they bring."[42] Thus, include a variety of elements to get the most out of your fab four team.

Famous groups of four include Blanche, Rose, Dorothy, and Sophia in *The Golden Girls*; the Beatles; the Fantastic Four; *South Park*'s kids; Kramer, George, Elaine, and Jerry in *Seinfeld*; and Dorothy, the Scarecrow, the Tin Man, and the Cowardly Lion in *The Wizard of Oz*.

Groups of Five People

With a group of five people, you'll either get the Dream Team or *Party of Five*. As you start adding people to any group, you have more chance for productivity to run off the rails. The 1992 Dream Team had a coach to guide these superstar players. And although rumors say the team (and coach) partied most of their time in Barcelona, when it was game time, they put it all on the court. The coach coordinated the players so that each could play their individual role the best among the other superstars. This is key to a successful group of five.

The group of five is best used for action-oriented activities. So long as different perspectives are used for brainstorming rather than division, this group can lead to creative solutions. While the group of four is relatively peaceful and harmonious at reaching a solution, the group of five is likely to be more raucous in their approach. This can make for a fun workday if there is camaraderie within the group. A group of five people can also bring enthusiasm to a project that needs a boost of energy.

A group of five people with each having their primary element in each of the five elements would be the ideal team. In doing so, each person can contribute their best skills to the project at hand. Of course, this may not be possible due to availability of people, and someone's primary element might not be immediately clear. However, by reading the element descriptions in chapter 4 and 5, you should have a generally good idea of what personality type fits certain people.

Although this may be a version of stereotyping, most people are hired or included in groups based on what skillsets they have to offer. Being true to what someone is best at should be adhered to for the greatest success of the person and the group. When someone is thrown into a position that doesn't fit them, it throws off their confidence, can lead to low morale in groups, and impacts the overall success of a project.

Famous groups of five include the Jackson 5, the Spice Girls, the *Scooby-Doo* ensemble, the Simpsons family, One Direction, and the *Party of Five* ensemble.

CHAPTER 14

Implementing the Five Elements Method in the Workplace

> When you are content to be simply yourself and
> don't compare or compete, everybody will respect you.
> —*Tao Te Ching*, translated by Stephen Mitchell

Over the span of my career, I have meandered through the corporate world as an attorney and the healing arts as an energy healer and everything in between. I use the word *meander* because it's a term of art used in feng shui that exemplifies the ideal path in which energy moves. Instead of rushing or stagnating, energy should meander in a snakelike shape like a natural-formed river. This is the shape of the yin-yang symbol formed from the integration of the two energies.

I've had many clients who've also been on this meandering career path integrating both the yang energy of the corporate world with the yin energy of the creative arts. These two energies within ourselves are striving to find expression, although it's typically the creative yin that doesn't get the time and space it prefers in our yang-driven culture. It can feel like an internal battle within us as these opposing energies strive to find balance. The solution is integration.

We see these opposing forces on a global level with ongoing cultural wars between the rights of men and women, between

Democrats and Republicans, and between the patriarchal and matriarchal. Political tensions mirror the polarization of yin and yang energy. The area in which we've seen an integration of yin yang energy is in gender nonconformity. The idea of not identifying with a gender, also referred to as nonbinary, is more prevalent among younger generations but gaining acceptance regardless of age. I expect this to continue until we essentially find a balanced integration—one that is a unification of yin and yang.

As the lines that make up our boxes and categories blur, it's then that we go beyond these dualistic parts of ourselves to become metahuman. As we find unification within ourselves, we also find that with others. The Taoist adage "We are all one" can become a more accepted reality. We can also apply these same principles to create holistic businesses that consider the entire ecosystem similar to biodynamic farming. While we each expand ourselves beyond a category for purposes of self-growth of our individual self, we also contribute to partnerships or groups to something bigger than ourselves.

As human beings, we're spiritual beings having a physical experience with a connection to the physical world and spirit world. We embody the duality of yin and yang with a left side, right side, left brain, and right brain creating an antenna of energy from the heavens, the unmanifest, to the earth, the manifest. We are the by-products of the creative process upon being birthed into the human experience. Thus, we are inherently creative beings ourselves. We create our reality daily, from the mundane to the extraordinary, by way of the Five Elements Cycle. It is in essence the prescription for creating things from thoughts.

Although you've been creating using the Five Elements all your life, you now have a conscious understanding of how this creative cycle works. You can now recognize which phase you're in and, more importantly, which phase you've neglected in the past. In the next section, you'll learn how to implement the Five Elements Cycle with more intention so that it becomes a regular part of your workflow.

The Five Elements Method

Most of our human challenges can be solved by looking to nature. This is the philosophy behind the practice of biomimicry. Similar to Taoism, the practice of biomimicry looks to the interconnectedness of all living things to create products, processes, and new ways of living by mimicking strategies found in nature. The Five Elements Cycle is a direct way to mimic the creative process found in nature. Our biorhythms and organ systems are naturally aligned with the Five Elements. Of course, this makes sense because we are also a part of nature. It's easy to think that we humans are separate and superior in hierarchy to other species on the planet, but we are all at the influence of the same energetic forces that created the planets, stars, and all living creatures. The more we surrender to the Tao, or the Way, of how energy flows with the Five Elements Cycle, the more we can create a win-win-win result: a win for you, a win for the recipient of your creation, and a win for the planet.

The Five Elements Method can be used as a method to assist you in creating in accordance with the Five Elements Cycle. While chapter 3 provided examples of using the Five Elements Cycle for creating a book, film, and other uses, you can use the Five Elements Method to assist you in your process for creating virtually anything. In other words, you've unlocked the formula to manifest on another level than ever before. Once you become familiar with the steps, it will become a part of your everyday workflow. The following chart shows the phases of the Five Elements Method to use for any project, including starting a business, as discussed in the next section.

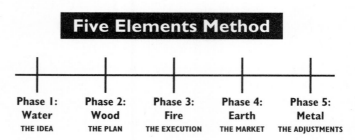

Figure 4. Five Elements Method

Five Elements Method for Solo Entrepreneurs and Creatives

If you're a solo business owner or someone who considers yourself to be a creative, then you have the task of orchestrating all five phases for the successful completion of what you're creating. Whether you decide to bring in other people for help or collaboration is an ongoing question for solo entrepreneurs. *How much can I really do on my own? How much do I want to do on my own?* The answers to these questions may depend on time or skill constraints regarding what you're capable of for the success of your business or individual project. Now that you have a clearer idea of where your strengths and weaknesses lie, you can make a more informed decision.

Is the learning curve of your missing element too time consuming and therefore not feasible to take on? Or perhaps your time is better spent executing your primary element. And yet always be open to the idea that your missing element may be the missing link, also known as your hidden strength, that will help uplevel your creative expression. For example, social media has never been my strong suit, especially videos. However, I recently discovered that the combination of the one-minute time constraint combined with the giving expert advice on TikTok is a sweet spot for me. I actually enjoy making these videos, and they have resulted in a number of great clients.

The Five Elements Method can be implemented for any short-term or long-term project for solo entrepreneurs. It's also a great formula to use in starting a business. A business starts with an idea to do something you enjoy, to express your talent and skills, or possibly a desire to effect some change in the world. It can also simply be for the purpose of making money, or a combination of all those reasons. Either way, it's your *why*. This is, of course, the Water element phase.

The next phase is the beginning stages of implementing your idea by creating a plan. You've likely heard that a business should start with a business plan. This is essential for obtaining a loan or some other form of financing from investors or crowdfunding. The business plan lays out the practical aspects of the business. At this point, you'll also make branding decisions and file the appropriate business filings. This is the Wood element phase.

From there, the Fire phase is where the pieces start to come together and gather momentum. You announce your business, start marketing and advertising, procure necessary supplies and any other resources, including contractors or employees. To stay committed through the Fire phase, your *why* in the Water phase must be strong enough to carry you through without burnout.

Depending on the nature of the business, a soft opening or beta test might be a better option before the official launch. After all, the Earth element phase is when you receive feedback from customers or the public. This could be in the form of surveys,

Chapter 14

social media hits, or early sales and reviews. You see how your product or service is landing on people. Based on this phase, you will make necessary adjustments in the Metal phase. Now that you have more information, you can edit your original idea and business plan, if needed. From here, you either go back to the phases that need more attention, or you launch into a new phase of the business and repeat the Five Elements Cycle, each time with more vigor, focus, clarity, and success.

When you consider all five phases as being essential to a business, it's no wonder why the average business takes two to three years to turn a profit.[43] In fact, according to the Bureau of Labor Statistics, approximately "20% of small businesses fail within the first year" and "30% of businesses fail in their second year," with an overall 70 percent failure rate.[44] With these statistics, it's important not to skip any of the phases of the Five Elements Cycle.

Think back to past business or creative ventures. Which phase did you skip or gloss over? Is there a phase that you get stuck in and can't seem to move from? Which phase is your favorite and where you thrive? These are all important questions to consider for the next time you create something new. You'll likely notice that your answers are mirrored in other areas of your life, from self-care practices, your health, and relationships.

The following worksheet is a basic outline or formula to follow. It can be used as a general guide and is changeable to fit your specific project or activity. I encourage you to write your answers in a notebook or journal to allow yourself space to expand your ideas and thoughts about your project.

Five Elements Method Worksheet

Project Title: _____

Step 1: Water—The Idea

What's your why? What's the internal motivation behind what you want to do?

I want to create _____

about _____

because I feel passionate about _____

_____ because

of my experience with _____

_____.

Additional Notes for Water Phase: _____

_____

_____

_____.

Step 2: Wood—The Plan

What's your plan (i.e., business plan, book outline, blueprint, prototype)?

I will create a plan that includes _____

_____ followed by _____

_____ with a goal of completion

by _____.

Additional Notes for Wood Phase: _____

_____

_____

_____.

Step 3: Fire—The Execution

How much time and energy are you willing to put into it?

I commit to working on _____ for
_____ hours/week for _____ months/
years in order to finish _____.

Additional Notes for Fire Phase: _____
_____
_____
_____.

Step 4: Earth—The Market

Whose problem am I solving and how will I let them know?

My target audience or customer is _____
_____ because it meets their need of
_____, and I will reach
them through the marketing channels of _____
_____ by sharing my personal story of
_____.

Additional Notes for Earth Phase: _____
_____
_____
_____.

Step 5: Metal—The Adjustments

What changes do I need to make from my original idea, if any?

After _____, I realize I need to
eliminate _____ from _____
_____.

I need to change _____

_____.

I can improve upon _____ if I take
out/change/add _____

_____.

I need to go back to the _____ phase so that I can

_____

_____.

Additional Notes for Metal Phase: _____

_____

_____

_____.

Worksheet Sample

Project Title: *Missing Element, Hidden Strength*

Water: I want to create <u>a nonfiction book</u> about <u>applying the ancient wisdom of the five elements to our modern work environment and creative process</u> because I feel passionate about <u>helping people and the planet create a win-win-win not only for continued survival but also for a higher level of enjoyment and satisfaction</u>.

Wood: I will create a plan that includes <u>a working chapter outline</u> followed by <u>a book proposal to pitch to agents or publishers</u> with a goal of completion by <u>April 30, 2022</u>.

Fire: I commit to working on <u>the book proposal</u> for <u>20</u> hours / week for <u>2</u> months in order to finish <u>the book proposal and sample chapters</u>.

Earth: My target audience or customer is <u>entrepreneurial-minded people who also appreciate spirituality</u> because it meets their need of <u>creating at their highest level for the purpose of greater achievement, success, and overall fulfillment,</u> and I will reach them through the marketing channels of <u>podcast interviews, workshops, speaking engagements, Instagram, and TikTok</u> by sharing my personal story of <u>how I use the Five Elements in my writing process as an author and how I've turned my missing element into my hidden strength</u>.

Metal: After <u>writing the first draft</u>, I realize I need to eliminate <u>nothing from my original outline, but I need to do heavy copyediting for the second draft</u>. I need to change <u>part 2 by including a separate chapter for each element instead of putting it all into one chapter</u>. I can improve upon <u>the Five Elements Method</u> if I <u>add a personal example</u>. I need to go back to the <u>Wood phase to adjust my outline and to the Fire phase to expand chapters 7 through 11 and also include the future of decentralization in the final chapter.</u>

Five Elements Method for Corporations and Managers

The Five Elements Method can also be beneficial in larger corporate settings. A corporation is the same as a single-owned business with its unique mission, or *why* statement, except its products or services reach a larger number of customers. Thus, more employees are needed to create the amount of output necessary. Employees are usually organized in a hierarchal structure with managers, also known as middle management, overseeing a certain amount of people. The middle managers usually report to upper management, or the officers, known as the C-suite (i.e., CEO, CFO, COO, etc.). The number of middle management ladders will depend on the size and business model of each company.

Corporations typically place employees in "teams" that are either function-based or product-based. If a team is function-based (for example, sales, legal, or finance), then each employee is going to be hired for a specific skillset, which in most cases is their primary element—at least that's what the hiring manager should hope for. Although it varies by corporation, the typical departments include strategy, marketing, finance, human resources, technology, and operations. The role for each of these departments varies greatly depending on services and products offered, however, in general, the departments fall in line with the Five Elements as follows:

Research and Development: Water or Metal element

Strategy: Water or Wood element

Operations: Wood or Fire element

Marketing: Wood or Fire element

Accounting and Finance: Earth or Metal element

Human Resources: Earth element

Technology: Metal element

For product-based teams, however, you're likely to have a combination of skillsets involved. This is where forming teams that replicate the Five Elements Cycle becomes advantageous. Anytime there is a process of creating something new, this sets the Five Elements Cycle into motion, as do improvements of the product. For example, at time of writing, Apple is up to version 13 of the iPhone and Ethereum cryptocurrency is already working on its 2.0 version, with each version being a spiral of expansion and innovation of the Five Elements Cycle.

In the case of product-based teams, placing a variety of element types on a team is recommended. In the same way that too many cooks can be in the kitchen, too many of any one element can be counterproductive when innovation is involved. Where an existing product or operation is being maintained, having a team with the same elements is effective and provides reliability and consistency. In forming teams, refer to chapter 13 to determine whether a team of three, four, or five people is preferred depending on the goal.

In the case of hiring employees, managers should consider using the Five Elements Quiz in determining a candidate's strengths. While other factors are considered in deciding whether to hire a candidate, the Five Elements Quiz can provide useful information for where the employee best fits within the corporation and on which team they would be the best fit. Keep in mind that the Five Elements profile does not place any person with a higher standing in proficiency or intellect than any other person.

The use of personality tests in the hiring process is on the rise. A reported 80 percent of Fortune 100 companies use them to build better teams, with Myers-Briggs test being the most used method.[45] I would expect the trend of using personality assessments to become commonplace among companies as remote working and hiring are on the rise. With fewer in-person encounters, what was once done intuitively based on basic personality traits must now be done remotely over the computer. Instead of casual conversations in the break room or in meetings, managers must rely on more formal ways of assessing one's personality traits and strengths.

The same is true among team members. Instead of the benefit of meeting in a conference room around a table with a whiteboard, team meetings now take place over Zoom in hybrid workplaces. For this reason, organizing the steps needed as provided in the following Five Elements Method worksheet can be a useful tool for the overall creation and execution of the project at hand. Also, consider delegating tasks in accordance with the Five Elements to streamline the tasks and optimize the talents of each element represented on the team.

Five Elements Method Worksheet (Corporate Teams)

Project Title: _____

Step 1: Water—The Idea

What's the why behind this project? How does this project fit within the corporate mission?

We want to create _____

_____ for the purpose of _____

_____ because the corporation's mission is

_____.

Team Members Assigned: _____

_____

_____

_____

Step 2: Wood—The Plan

What's the plan (i.e., business plan, book outline, blueprint, prototype)?

Our plan includes _____

_____ followed by _____

_____with a goal of completion by

_____.

Team Members Assigned: _____

_____

_____

_____

Step 3: Fire—The Execution

What time allotment is needed for execution of the project?

This project will take a total _____ months/years in order to finish with execution of the plan performed by _____
_____.

Additional Notes for Fire Phase: _____
_____
_____
_____
_____

Step 4: Earth—The Market

Whose problem are we solving for whom?

Our target audience or customer is _____
_____ because it meets their need of _____
_____ and we will reach them
through these marketing channels: _____
_____.

Team Members Assigned: _____
_____
_____
_____

Step 5: Metal—The Adjustments

What changes are needed from the original idea, if any?

After _____, we need to change _____

_____.

We can improve the original design if we take out/change/add

_____

_____.

Team Members Assigned: _____

_____

_____

_____

Creating a Holistic Work Model

Imagine a world in which the Five Elements were integrated into all businesses and corporations. It's already being done aesthetically as businesses realize the importance of space and its effect on employee retention, not to mention sales. Call it feng shui, environmental design, or simply keeping the plants alive in the lobby, these models based on nature are being integrated more and more into our environments.

Businesses are also realizing the need for a more holistic environment by providing meditation, yoga, fitness, and other lifestyle classes to support their employees' overall well-being. The need for a holistic model is becoming the norm. After the COVID-19 epidemic, the need for a holistic environment is even more accentuated. No longer is the use of space for utilitarian purposes, or even a recruitment tool, but a life support system for employees.

The closer we mimic nature in all that we do, the more successful we will be. This includes considering the entire ecosystem, from employees to the community to the land to the products and services provided. We must move toward a win-win-win paradigm where all involved win, including planet earth.

The Future Tao

The *Tao Te Ching* is still used as a reference tool for the qualities that make up a good leader. The predominant theme is that one should lead not from the ego, but for what's best for the group. For example, the *Tao* states, "When the Master governs, the people are hardly aware that he exists."[46] This approach to leading is much aligned with the idea of decentralization, which is becoming a buzzword in areas of banking, finance, and commerce, along with push back from those in power.

Decentralization is the process by which an organization distributes decision-making away from a central, authoritarian person or group. An *Entrepreneur* magazine article states that the pandemic has quickened the trend toward decentralization as consumers and employees demand more control.[47] Additionally, remote work environments have prompted the need for more decentralization in workplace management. The days of a micromanaging boss breathing down our neck may be over as we move toward more Taoistic approaches.

Today's management could learn from the wisdom provided in the *Tao Te Ching*, including the following: "The master does his job and then stops. He understands that the universe is forever out of control, and that trying to dominate events goes against the current of the Tao. Because he believes in himself, he doesn't try to convince others. Because he is content with himself, he doesn't need others' approval. Because he accepts himself, the whole world accepts him."[48] As decentralization expands into the workplace, it also moves the burden of sovereignty over oneself onto the employees. In this case, it's more important than ever to embrace all Five Elements within oneself. That means turning your missing element into your hidden strength.

Conclusion

I magine where you'll be speaking. What show you'll appear on. On which podcasts you'll be a guest." The instructor guided us through a meditation to visualize the success of our future book. It was working, I felt like I was really on stage. But as I looked out into the crowd, all I could see was a huge mirror reflecting a blinding light. It was the kind of mirror used in feng shui to push energy away from itself, but only it was gigantic. As I stood there on stage with thousands of people looking at me, the lights, the cameras, the giant mirror—it was all too much. I opened my eyes. I was sitting among the other workshop participants who were also planting seeds for their future books.

This book was conceived at that writing workshop in Ojai only a couple months before the COVID-19 pandemic hit. When asked to come up with a word or intention for the weekend, I wrote *inception*. I looked up its exact meaning: beginning of a new system. That weekend was also the beginning of realizing I had work to do before this book could be released into the world. On myself. If I were to write a book on upleveling your life and work, then I would need to do it for myself. More importantly, I would need to go into the proverbial cave to face my missing element in order to actualize my hidden strength.

The meditation gave me my first big clue to where my fears were lurking. On stage. Under the lights. Being seen. I was initially confused because public speaking was nothing new for me. In school, speaking came rather naturally. I never broke out in hives or sweats or had an embarrassing moment on stage. As you read in the introduction, I made it through my role in *The Hobbit* in sixth grade. Professionally, I've been a guest on numerous TV shows and nothing has gone terribly wrong. So why was this imaginary stage so scary? As I replayed the meditation scene in my mind, I realized the fear was me being on stage *by myself.* And the larger the crowd, the larger the mirror.

Following that weekend workshop, a string of unfortunate events happened. It was as if this vision set into motion all the blocks and obstacles I would need to overcome in order to manifest a new level of success. As I rolled back in town from the workshop, I stopped at Whole Foods in preparation for the next morning's coffee. As I was backing out, I rammed into a 2020 black Audi Q7. This was right after my brand-new MacBook Pro completely crashed that morning. A few days later, I had a scheduled dermatological treatment to laser the epidermis from my face as a cancer prevention technique. As I sat there with the gazillion degree laser light frying my face with eye-protective goggles, I imagined being on that stage with the light brightly shining on me, being seen, and being okay.

As my face healed over the next few days, a rash simultaneously appeared along my rib cage. I figured I had an allergic reaction to something, but as the rash intensified, Dr. Google diagnosed it as shingles. This began a pain-filled three weeks of glass shards stabbing into me, which were followed by another four weeks of severe vertigo symptoms from neurological damage. The whole ordeal ended up being a two-month event of not moving. Between the pain of the shingles and the vertigo, I was limited to meditating, listening to audiobooks, and watching romantic comedies. Ironically, as soon as my symptoms cleared, the world went into quarantine, with stillness being the new world order for everyone. Because I had mastered the art of going nowhere, I had no problem adjusting to the new lifestyle.

As a firm believer in mind-body medicine, I knew the shingles had a message for me, and given the two months of stillness, I was in a place to listen. The shingles represented the roof that I'd hit, my upper limit. Like a real-life video game, I had mastered the level I'd been at, and it was time for a new level. It was time to integrate my missing element, the Fire element, so that it would no longer need to manifest in the form of a rash or other anger-provoking situations. Anytime we experience too much of an element, we're naturally thrown into its opposite. In this case, I was put into timeout in the Water element to cool off and sit with unprocessed grief. Nature does this too. Following wildfires comes the flood. Extremism occurs when imbalances pervade.

This imbalance of the Fire element had been keeping me at a certain level of success. More importantly, it was keeping me at a dulled level of happiness and satisfaction in every area of my life. The Fire element is the element, not only of our life force energy and visibility, but also where we find joy and play, an area of life which I was sorely missing. Depending on which element is missing for you, you too are living a half-lived life in some area and perhaps keeping the bar low as to the level of success and happiness of which you're capable.

For example, it could be the emotional and creative depths of the Water element that you've feared, and you've only skimmed the surface of the spiritual connection within yourself and others. If your Wood element has become too pruned, then you may be missing out on seeing a bigger vision and plan for yourself. Or maybe your Earth element is missing. If so, you've been missing out on properly nurturing or taking care of yourself, in relationships, projects, or money. Or perhaps you've given up on completing projects altogether to avoid your Metal element. Is your inner critic so loud that it prevents you from finishing projects or starting them altogether?

Do you want to just get by, or do you want to fly? This was my realization when I hit my ceiling. I was doing well, but I wasn't thriving. More importantly, I was lacking a level of joy that I knew was attainable. And then on a Friday afternoon in September, I got one of those calls you never want to get. My brother-in-law of thirty years had died suddenly of a pulmonary embolism at age fifty-three.

As the days, weeks, and months of shock settled in, everything in my life was put into perspective. I realized I want to make the most of each day. I want to live life to the fullest, experiencing it in the deepest way possible without the need to be or fear of being seen. I want to appreciate everyone and everything in my life. That's what it means to embrace not only the Fire element but all the elements. Sometimes life shows us what we don't want in order to wholeheartedly claim what we do want. Embracing my missing element meant embracing my whole Self. And that's the secret to your hidden strength.

It is my hope that you find the deepest fulfillment possible in this lifetime. This book is not meant to change you but to help you become more of who you already are. I have no doubt that your missing element—the part that you've hidden from the world—is your hidden strength and that your best is yet to come.

Acknowledgments

This book was birthed during the time we'll always remember as quarantine. History shows that great art comes from such times. While I'm not sure this book qualifies as that, I am proud to have written it during this historical moment and hope it can be a positive voice to the new consciousness on our planet.

Writing has always been my go-to during difficult times, and so I'm especially grateful to Angela Wix and the team at Llewellyn for saying yes to this book. I appreciate the collaboration and teamwork you continue to provide to the creative process.

I want to thank my writing group that kept me on course during all phases of this book. I know my job was to support their writing journey, but in this case, the teacher was the student. I formed not only a writing group, but a community of women I call my friends. Thank you to Kellen Brugman, Jennifer Rawls, Jean Hodgson, Jill Austin, Traci Smith, Tatiana Cameron, Rachael Cohen, Andrea Visser, and Dez Stephens for being there each week.

Thank you to Zhena Muzyka for opening the Magic Hour space just in time to spill your magic onto this book. You saw its potential and gave me the confirmation I needed to fully commit.

I have a heart full of gratitude for my wife, Rachel, who gives me the extra Fire I need each day, while graciously receiving my Metal. Together, with our Water and Wood, we will continue building our dreams on this Earth.

And, finally, to you, the reader. Thank you. You may have noticed stories from my childhood throughout the book. It was in fact a nostalgic time for a crabby Cancer sign stuck at home with a lot of self-reflection from the past. My hope is that those stories will help you gather the tools from your youth and leap you forward into your expanded self, and together we create a world that lives in harmony with each other and planet Earth for a win-win-win.

Endnotes

1. Joseph Campbell, *A Joseph Campbell Companion: Reflections on the Art of Living*, ed. Diane K. Osbon (New York: HarperCollins, 1991), 24.

2. Hu-Ching Ni, *The Taoist Inner View of the Universe and Immortal Realm* (Los Angeles, CA: Sevenstar Communications, 1979), preface.

3. Harriet Beinfield and Efrem Korngold, *Between Heaven and Earth: A Guide to Chinese Medicine* (New York: Ballantine Books, 1991), 5.

4. Ni, *The Taoist Inner View of the Universe and Immortal Realm*, preface.

5. Confucius, *The Analects of Confucius: A Philosophical Translation*, trans. Roger T. Ames and Henry Rosemont Jr. (New York: Ballantine Books, 1999), 27.

6. Joan Didion, "Why I Write," *New York Times*, December 5, 1976.

7. Anne Lamott, *Bird by Bird: Some Instructions on Writing and Life* (New York: Anchor, 1995), 20.

8. Julia Cameron, *The Artist's Way: A Spiritual Path to Higher Creativity* (New York: Putnam, 1996), 153.

9. For a more detailed discussion on Chinese Medicine principles as it relates to physical health, see Harriet Beinfield and Efrem Korngold, *Between Heaven and Earth* (New York: Ballantine Books, 1991).

10. Beinfield and Korngold, *Between Heaven and Earth*, 134.

11. Eben Harrell, "A Brief History of Personality Tests," *Harvard Business Review*, March–April 2017, https://hbr.org/2017/03/a-brief-history-of-personality-tests.

12. Harrell, "A Brief History of Personality Tests."

13. Harrell, "A Brief History of Personality Tests."

14. James Hollis, *The Middle Passage: From Misery to Meaning in Midlife* (Toronto: Inner City Books, 1993), 73.

15. Craig Gustafson, "Bruce Lipton, PhD: The Jump from Cell Culture to Consciousness," *Integrative Medicine: A Clinician's Journal* 16, no. 6 (December 2017): 48.

16. Gustafson, "Bruce Lipton, PhD," 49.

17. Anna Johansson, "7 Ways Your Office Affects Productivity (Without Your Realizing It)," *Entrepreneur*, November 14, 2018, https://www.entrepreneur.com/article/322504.

18. This is the case for home offices that share space with a guest bedroom. In most cases, the guest bed ends up taking the power position rather than the desk. I have no problem with prioritizing guests over work, especially if I'm your guest, so long as it's a conscious choice to do so.

19. Hollis, *The Middle Passage,* 77.

20. James Clear, *Atomic Habits* (New York: Random House, 2018), 143.

21. Ephrat Livni, "Albert Einstein's Best Ideas Came When He Was Aimless. Yours Can Too," Quartz, June 8, 2018, https://qz.com/1299282/albert-einsteins-best-ideas-came-while-he-was-relaxing-aimlessly-yours-can-too/; "Auction 108: Letters by A. Einstein," Winner's Auctions, accessed March 9, 2022, https://winners-auctions.com/en/items/where-does-albert-einstein-find-refuge-calm-and-serenity/.

22. Nikola Tesla, "Some Personal Recollections: An Autobiographical Sketch," *Scientific American* 112, no. 23 (June 5, 1915): 576, https://www.jstor.org/stable/26022227.

23. Nikola Tesla, *My Inventions: The Autobiography of Nikola Tesla* (New York: Electrical Experimenter, 1919; repr., Eastford, CT: Martino Fine Books, 2018), 28.

24. Olivia Goldhill, "Psychologists Recommend Children Be Bored in the Summer," Quartz, last modified June 14, 2019, https://qz.com/704723/to-be-more-self-reliant-children-need-boring-summers/.

25. Stephanie McMains and Sabine Kastner, "Interactions of Top-Down and Bottom-Up Mechanisms in Human Visual Cortex," *Journal of Neuroscience* 31, no. 2 (January 2011): 587–97, https://doi.org/10.1523/JNEUROSCI.3766-10.2011.

26. Tracee Stanley, *Radiant Rest: Yoga Nidra for Deep Relaxation and Awakened Clarity* (Boulder, CO: Shambhala, 2021).

27. Cameron, *The Artist's Way*, 9.

28. Victoria Turk, "How to Use Office Plants to Boost Productivity and Job Satisfaction," *Wired*, November 24, 2017, https://www.wired.co.uk/article/office-plants-boost-productivity.

29. Centers for Disease Control and Prevention, "More People Walk to Better Health," August 2012, https://www.cdc.gov /vitalsigns/walking/.

30. Valter Longo, "What Exercise Is Best for Optimal Health and Longevity," Blue Zones, accessed December 21, 2021, https:// www.bluezones.com/2018/01/what-exercise-best-happy -healthy-life/.

31. Mohamed Boubekri, Ivy N. Cheung, Kathryn J. Reid, Chia-Hui Wang, and Phyllis C. Zee, "Impact of Windows and Daylight Exposure on Overall Health and Sleep Quality of Office Workers," *Journal of Clinical Sleep Medicine* 10, no. 6 (June 15, 2014), 603, https://www.ncbi.nlm.nih.gov/pmc/articles /PMC4031400/.

32. Jeanne C. Meister, "The #1 Office Perk? Natural Light," *Harvard Business Review*, September 3, 2018, https://hbr.org/2018 /09/the-1-office-perk-natural-light.

33. Walbert Castillo, "How to Dress for a Job Interview," Huff-Post, November 19, 2014, https://www.huffpost.com/entry /how-to-dress-for-a-job-in_b_5844868.

34. Oprah Winfrey, *Oprah's Super Soul,* OWN Podcasts, podcast, MP3 audio, https://podcasts.apple.com/us/podcast/oprahs -super-soul/id1264843400?mt=2.

35. Ram Dass and Mirabai Bush, *Walking Each Other Home: Conversations on Loving and Dying* (Boulder, CO: Sounds True, 2018).

36. Marie Kondo, *The Life-Changing Magic of Tidying Up: The Japanese Art of Decluttering and Organizing,* trans. Cathy Hirano (New York: Ten Speed Press, 2014).

37. Andy Greene, "Bernie Taupin on 48 Years Writing with Elton John and Their New LP," *Rolling Stone*, November 17, 2015, https://www.rollingstone.com/music/music-news/bernie-taupin-on-48-years-writing-with-elton-john-and-their-new-lp-59194/.

38. Ray Dalio, *Principles: Life and Work* (New York: Simon & Schuster, 2017), 368.

39. Gene Hammett, "The 3 Elements of Successful Business Partnerships," *Inc.*, January 25, 2019, https://www.inc.com/gene-hammett/the-3-elements-of-successful-business-partnerships.html.

40. Hammett, "The 3 Elements of Successful Business Partnerships."

41. Dalio, *Principles*, 368–9.

42. Dalio, *Principles*, 423.

43. Gene Marks, "Want to Turn Huge Startup Profits? Here's Why You Need to Be Patient," *Entrepreneur*, October 18, 2013, https://www.entrepreneur.com/article/229499.

44. Georgia McIntyre, "What Percentage of Small Businesses Fail? (and Other Need-to-Know Stats)," Fundera, last modified November 20, 2020, https://www.fundera.com/blog/what-percentage-of-small-businesses-fail.

45. Elena Bajic, "How the MBTI Can Help You Build a Stronger Company," *Forbes*, September 28, 2015, https://www.forbes.com/sites/elenabajic/2015/09/28/how-the-mbti-can-help-you-build-a-stronger-company/?sh=7decf555d93c.

46. Lao Tzu, *Tao Te Ching*, trans. Stephen Mitchell (New York: Harper Perennial, 1994), number 17.

47. Pritom Das, "5 Decentralization Trends to Watch in 2020," *Entrepreneur*, April 27, 2020, https://www.entrepreneur.com /article/347994.

48. Lao Tzu, *Tao Te Ching*, trans. Mitchell, number 30.

Bibliography

Bajic, Elena. "How the MBTI Can Help You Build a Stronger Company," *Forbes*, September 28, 2015. https://www.forbes.com/sites/elenabajic/2015/09/28/how-the-mbti-can-help-you-build-a-stronger-company/?sh=7decf555d93c.

Beinfield, Harriet, and Efrem Korngold. *Between Heaven and Earth: A Guide to Chinese Medicine*. New York: Ballantine Books, 1991.

Boubekri, Mohamed, Ivy N. Cheung, Kathryn J. Reid, Chia-Hui Wang, and Phyllis C. Zee. "Impact of Windows and Daylight Exposure on Overall Health and Sleep Quality of Office Workers." *Journal of Clinical Sleep Medicine* 10, no. 6 (June 15, 2014), 603–11. https://www.ncbi.nlm.nih.gov/pmc/articles/PMC4031400/.

Bukowski, Charles. *What Matters Most Is How Well You Walk Through the Fire*. Ecco, 2002

Brown, Brené. *Dare to Lead: Brave Work. Tough Conversations. Whole Hearts*. New York: Random House, 2018.

Cameron, Julia. *The Artist's Way: A Spiritual Path to Higher Creativity*. New York: Putnam, 1996.

Campbell, Joseph. *A Joseph Campbell Companion: Reflections on the Art of Living*. Edited by Diane K. Osbon. New York: HarperCollins, 1991.

Bibliography

Castillo, Walbert. "How to Dress for a Job Interview." HuffPost. November 19, 2014. https://www.huffpost.com/entry/how -to-dress-for-a-job-in_b_5844868.

Centers for Disease Control and Prevention. "More People Walk to Better Health." August, 2012. https://www.cdc.gov/vitalsigns /walking/.

Clear, James. *Atomic Habits*. New York: Random House, 2018.

Confucius. *The Analects of Confucius: A Philosophical Translation*. Translated by Roger T. Ames and Henry Rosemont Jr. New York: Ballantine Books, 1999.

Dalio, Ray. *Principles: Life and Work*. New York: Simon & Schuster, 2017.

Das, Pritom. "5 Decentralization Trends to Watch in 2020." *Entrepreneur*, April 27, 2020. https://www.entrepreneur.com/article /347994.

Dass, Ram, and Bush, Mirabai. *Walking Each Other Home: Conversations on Loving and Dying*. Boulder, CO: Sounds True, 2018.

Didion, Joan. "Why I Write." *New York Times,* December 5, 1976.

Eames, Charles. *100 Quotes by Charles Eames*. Los Angeles: Eames Office, 2007.

Gandhi, Mahatma. *The Essential Gandhi: An Anthology of His Writings on His Life, Work, and Ideas*. Edited by Louis Fischer. New York: Vintage Spiritual Classics, 1962.

Goldhill, Olivia. "Psychologists Recommend Children Be Bored in the Summer." Quartz. Last modified June 14, 2019. https:// qz.com/704723/to-be-more-self-reliant-children-need -boring-summers/.

Greene, Andy. "Bernie Taupin on 48 Years Writing with Elton John and Their New LP." *Rolling Stone*, November 17, 2015. https://www.rollingstone.com/music/music-news/bernie-taupin-on-48-years-writing-with-elton-john-and-their-new-lp-59194/.

Gustafson, Craig. "Bruce Lipton, PhD: The Jump from Cell Culture to Consciousness." *Integrative Medicine: A Clinician's Journal* 16, no. 6 (December 2017): 45–50. https://www.ncbi.nlm.nih.gov/pmc/articles/PMC6438088/.

Hammett, Gene. "The 3 Elements of Successful Business Partnerships." *Inc. Magazine*, January 25, 2019. https://www.inc.com/gene-hammett/the-3-elements-of-successful-business-partnerships.html.

Harrell, Eben. "A Brief History of Personality Tests." *Harvard Business Review,* March–April 2017. https://hbr.org/2017/03/a-brief-history-of-personality-tests.

Hollis, James. *The Middle Passage: From Misery to Meaning in Midlife.* Toronto: Inner City Books, 1993.

Johansson, Anna. "7 Ways Your Office Affects Productivity (without Your Realizing It)." *Entrepreneur.* November 14, 2018. https://www.entrepreneur.com/article/322504.

Kondo, Marie. *The Life-Changing Magic of Tidying Up: The Japanese Art of Decluttering and Organizing.* Translated by Cathy Hirano. New York: Ten Speed Press, 2014.

Lamott, Anne. *Bird by Bird: Some Instructions on Writing and Life.* New York: Anchor, 1995.

Longo, Valter. "What Exercise is Best for Optimal Health and Longevity." Blue Zones. Accessed December 21, 2021. https://www.bluezones.com/2018/01/what-exercise-best-happy-healthy-life/.

Lao Tzu. *Tao Te Ching*. Translated by Arthur Waley. Ware, England: Wordsworth Editions, 1996.

———. *Tao Te Ching*. Translated by Gia-fu Feng and Jane English. New York: Vintage Books, 1997.

———. *Tao Te Ching*. Translated by Stephen Mitchell. New York: Harper Perennial, 1994.

Livni, Ephrat. "Albert Einstein's Best Ideas Came When He Was Aimless. Yours Can Too." Quartz, June 8, 2018. https://qz.com/1299282/albert-einsteins-best-ideas-came-while-he-was-relaxing-aimlessly-yours-can-too/.

Marks, Gene. "Want to Turn Huge Startup Profits? Here's Why You Need to Be Patient." *Entrepreneur*, October 18, 2013. https://www.entrepreneur.com/article/229499.

McIntyre, Georgia. "What Percentage of Small Businesses Fail? (And Other Need-to-Know Stats)." Fundera. Last modified November 20, 2020. https://www.fundera.com/blog/what-percentage-of-small-businesses-fail.

McMains, Stephanie, and Sabine Kastner. "Interactions of Top-Down and Bottom-Up Mechanisms in Human Visual Cortex." *Journal of Neuroscience* 31, no. 2 (January, 2011): 587–97. https://doi.org/10.1523/JNEUROSCI.3766-10.2011.

Meister, Jeanne C. "The #1 Office Perk? Natural Light." *Harvard Business Review*, September 3, 2018. https://hbr.org/2018/09/the-1-office-perk-natural-light.

Ni, Hu-Ching. *The Taoist Inner View of the Universe and Immortal Realm*. Los Angeles, CA: Sevenstar Communications, 1979.

Oliver, Mary. *West Wind: Poems and Prose Poems*. New York: Mariner Books, 1997.

Rilke, Rainer Maria. *Letters to a Young Poet*. Translated by Charlie Louth. London: Penguin Classics, 2016.

Tesla, Nikola. *My Inventions: The Autobiography of Nikola Tesla*. New York: Electrical Experimenter, 1919. Reprint, Eastford, CT: Martino Fine Books, 2018.

———. "Some Personal Recollections: An Autobiographical Sketch." *Scientific American* 112, no. 23 (June 5, 1915): 537, 576–577. https://www.jstor.org/stable/26022227.

Turk, Victoria. "How to Use Office Plants to Boost Productivity and Job Satisfaction." *Wired*, November 24, 2017. https://www.wired.co.uk/article/office-plants-boost-productivity.

Stanley, Tracee. *Radiant Rest: Yoga Nidra for Deep Relaxation and Awakened Clarity*. Boulder, CO: Shambhala, 2021.

Stidger, William L. "Ford Explains His 'Curio Shop' of America." *Detroit Times*, February 26, 1928.

Winfrey, Oprah. *Oprah's Super Soul*. OWN Podcasts. Podcast. MP3 audio. https://podcasts.apple.com/us/podcast/oprahs-super-soul/id1264843400?mt=2.

To Write to the Author

If you wish to contact the author or would like more information about this book, please write to the author in care of Llewellyn Worldwide Ltd. and we will forward your request. Both the author and the publisher appreciate hearing from you and learning of your enjoyment of this book and how it has helped you. Llewellyn Worldwide Ltd. cannot guarantee that every letter written to the author can be answered, but all will be forwarded. Please write to:

Tisha Morris
℅ Llewellyn Worldwide
2143 Wooddale Drive
Woodbury, MN 55125-2989
Please enclose a self-addressed stamped envelope for reply,
or $1.00 to cover costs. If outside the U.S.A., enclose
an international postal reply coupon.

Many of Llewellyn's authors have websites with additional information and resources. For more information, please visit our website at http://www.llewellyn.com.